A Practical Guide to

Designing
with Data

by Brian Suda

A Practical Guide to Designing with Data
by Brian Suda

Published in 2010 by Five Simple Steps
Studio Two, The Coach House
Stanwell Road
Penarth
CF64 3EU
United Kingdom

On the web: *www.fivesimplesteps.com*
and: *www.designingwithdata.com*
Please send errors to *errata@fivesimplesteps.com*

Publisher: Five Simple Steps
Editor: Owen Gregory
Production Editor: Emma Boulton
Art Director: Mark Boulton
Designer: Nick Boulton
Printed in the UK by Paramount Print

ISBN: 978-1-907828-02-7

A catalogue record of this book is available from the British Library.

FOREWORD

Jeremy Keith

I have known Brian Suda for many years. We first met through the microformats community, where he uses his skills to make structured data readily available and easily understandable. Now he is applying those skills to the world of data.

I am covetous of Brian's mind. It is the mind of a scientist, constantly asking questions: "What was the first man-made object with a unique identifier?", "What would a hypercube of bread classification look like?", "What would it sound like to say all fifty of the United States at the same time?"

Okay, that last one was from Family Guy. But whereas you or I would be content to laugh at the joke and move on, Brian actually tried it by layering fifty audio recordings on top of one another. For the record, it sounds like this: Mwashomomakota.

As you would expect from such an enquiring mind, this book is not a shallow overview of graphs and charts. If you are looking for a quick fix on how to make your PowerPoint presentations pop, this isn't the book for you. But if you want to understand what happens when the human brain interacts with representations of data, you have hit the motherlode.

It isn't hyperbole to say that this book will change the way you look at the world. In the same way that typography geeks can't help but notice the good and bad points of lettering in everyday life, you're going to start spotting data design all around you.

Better still, you are going to learn how to apply that deep knowledge to your own work. You will begin asking questions of yourself: "Am I communicating data honestly and effectively?", "What is the cognitive overhead of the information I am presenting?"

Your mind will be more Suda-like once you have read this book. The phrase "change your mind" is usually used to mean "reverse a decision". I want to use the phrase in a different, more literal way.

This book will change your mind.

Contents

INTRODUCTION

Over the years, I have been digging through large data sets both for work and pleasure. I love numbers, charts, graphs, visualizations, zeitgeists, raumzeitgeists, infographics and old maps. Getting to peek into what companies like Google get to see on a daily basis – trends, fads, search volume, relatedness, all bundled up in an interesting illustration – makes my day. Some people re-read the same book over and over; I can stare at a dense illustration and re-read its story. It makes me ask, "What caused these numbers? Where did they all come from?" It has been estimated that the Large Hadron Collider produces fifteen petabytes (fifteen million gigabytes) of data a year. It's impossible to look at a table of fifteen petabytes of information – there has to be a graphical representation for anyone to comprehend data at this volume.

This is what excites me: the challenge of how to take these boring numbers and design something more compelling. To tell the story behind the data, we need to stop grasping for the perfect visualization and instead return to the basic language of charts and graphs. Only then can we begin to uncover the meaning and relationships the data has to offer.

Beyond the basic bar charts and line graphs taught in schools, a new breed of illustrations has recently appeared. These new 'visualizations' are an attempt to explain the underlying information with a powerful visual impact. They take complex ideas and distil them into beautiful graphics revealing the interrelationships in the data. Some are so brilliantly executed that there are now annual awards for newspaper and magazine infographics to highlight their achievements. Sadly, over recent years terms such as visualization and infographic have been bandied around with almost no regard to their proper use or meaning. Existing chart types and even slide shows have been saddled with the more gratuitous term 'infographs' to sound more impressive. There is a new vernacular in the realm of data representation, but that doesn't mean we should ignore the underlying principles and best practices of humble charts and graphs. Once you have mastered the basics, more complex designs and visualizations become easier to create.

I wrote this book because I feel that people aren't taking the fundamentals of graphs and charts seriously. Many people are inspired by fancy visualizations and jump right in over their heads. As with any discipline, you need to put in the hard work by starting from the beginning.

If you look at publishers' catalogues, there are plenty of books on this topic, but they all cover somewhat esoteric aspects of specific charts and graphs: either from an academic point of view, stating how to right align numeric values or calculate confidence intervals to two standard deviations; or illustrated guides to beautiful posters and the information they represent. While these topics are certainly important, you need to consider the data's context and the readers who are looking to your charts and graphs for answers. Having a beautiful poster or a well documented confidence interval is worthless if the rest of the design is unreadable. I wrote this book in an attempt to distil as much knowledge as possible into just the information you will need day-to-day. There are plenty of specific kinds of charts for very specialized fields, from financial to weather data and everything in between, but they all require a fundamental understanding of the basics. Just because someone might be an expert in their field doesn't mean that they have the know-how to design with data.

This book is a peek into the pinball machine of my mind, always bouncing around various related and sometimes unrelated topics. I wanted to draw together several techniques you can use in your charts and graphs, such as how to minimize the number of pixels, and at the same time explain some interesting aspects of colour in our lives. In addition, I felt it was important to explain how to spot bad or misleading design: the kind that unscrupulous people use to trick us into believing their interpretation of data rather than the facts. Only then can you properly focus on the data, bypass unnecessary distractions and avoid misrepresenting the information.

The main purpose of this book is to encourage you to visualize and design for data in such a way that it engages the reader and tells a story rather than just being flashy, cluttered and confusing. Much like authors choose their words, sentences and paragraphs to structure ideas, informaticians have a bevy of concepts at their disposal to tell stories with data. What I want to focus on are best practices. These pages don't describe the one true way to design with data, but set out some guiding principles you can have at your disposal when you sit down and illustrate data.

The Five Simple Steps team has been great during this whole process. They let me write the book I wanted to write and were incredibly patient with my digressions. I hope that some of them help explain my thought processes as well as entertain with some interesting tidbits now and then. The five in Five Simple Steps is a great constraint for a writer, but it does mean that this is hardly a complete list of types of graphs and charts. New ideas and concepts are always appearing, some good, some bad. Instead of following an endless trail, this is an overview of the common types you'll run into on a regular basis and how to push them to get the maximum value.

The title *Designing with data* was chosen because I wanted to focus not on data collection, statistics or other mathematical analysis, but rather on the visualization of data. Much like you create a narrative in words, illustrations of data need to tell a story. How you go about designing with data is just about as open as how to write a book. The one thing we do know is that it is important to get the basics right. This book is an introduction to those basics and an invitation to you to become the next expert data designer.

Part 1

The visual language of data

Whether writing words, sketching a cartoon or illustrating a graph, you are telling a story to the reader. We all know the emotional power of a good book. The words on paper allow you to get sucked into the characters and plot. Classic paintings do the same. Millions of people go to see the Mona Lisa every year. Her eyes, her smile tell us a mysterious story. Who is she? The oil painting draws us into another world that we are welcome to explore. An effective illustration must do the same.

This book is about designing with data. Charts, graphs and other data visualizations have a language of their own. They convey meaning and information that is not available in words while demonstrating relationships within the data, and they allow the reader to make projections and better grasp the concepts. We need to learn how to tell a story with data and how to design it in such a way that it is no different than a great work of art or a bedtime story you remember from childhood. Well designed data should provoke emotions, tell a story, draw the reader in and let them explore.

Graph genesis

Chart literacy

Dynamic and static charts

Does this make me look fat?

Chart junk

GRAPH GENESIS

Some of the objects we use in our daily lives are so ubiquitous that we assume they have been around for all time. Even something as simple as the humble directional arrow, pointing the way and giving us instructions, once didn't exist. It was 'invented' for its modern day use. The barcode is a very modern invention (first conceived in the late 1940s but not widely used until the 1970s), yet we see it everywhere. One day, children will never have known a world without e-mail, the Internet or 3-D projection televisions.

In this book, I address the common types of charts and graphs, discuss some uncommon types and the reasons why they should stay that way. It's also important to look back at how many of these creations started off. As we'll see, they weren't so different than the charts we use today – two hundred years on and not much has changed. It makes you wonder, were charts and graphs invented or simply discovered? Were they destined to arrive in the form they did or are they so useful and near-perfect that we have just stuck with them?

Believe it or not, there once was a time before graphs and charts – they too were invented. The ancient Egyptians didn't have PowerPoint® presentations or pie charts (probably they also lived in blissful ignorance of a world of bulleted lists). Socrates taught his followers without the use of bar charts or Venn diagrams. Even the Romans didn't use graphs to visualize their luxurious spending sprees over the years, or miles of new roads constructed throughout the empire. Yet we assume that we can't live without three-dimensional quarterly projections from Excel®.

If we look back to the time when some of the very first charts were created, we'll see that they were born out of the need to explain large amounts of financial, political and social data. It wasn't until William Playfair (1759–1823), a Scottish engineer and political economist, published *The Commercial and Political Atlas* in 1786 and *Statistical Breviary* in 1801 that many of our modern visual devices for data first saw the light of day. He is credited with inventing the bar chart, line chart, pie chart and circle graph (see part 4).

Though Playfair gets most of the credit for kicking off this revolution, there are several other notable contributors who developed the tools we use today. You might know Joseph Priestley as 'the inventor of air'. Priestley was born in 1733 in England where he spent his life until 1791, when he fled persecution to the newly established USA. In 1765, he published *A Chart of Biography* which outlined the years of births and deaths of "statesmen of learning". This is one of the first timelines showing relative length and durations as a chart rather than as a table.

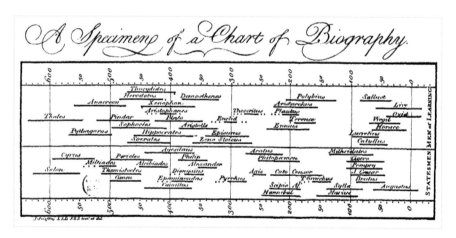

About twenty years after Priestley, in 1786, William Playfair published some of the first extant visual charts and graphs in his books about economics. Priestley's timeline certainly had an effect on Playfair as he created the bar charts. It is likely that William Playfair was aware of Priestley through various channels: the publication of Priestley's papers and books, almost certainly, but possibly also through the University of Edinburgh, which conferred the degree of Doctor of Law on Priestley in 1764. The Playfair family designed some of the most notable buildings of Edinburgh and its university, along with being deeply involved in the Enlightenment movement, as was Priestley.

Another contribution to the visualization of large sets of data came from Charles Dupin (1784–1873), a French mathematician and engineer. His contribution to the advancement of charts was the choropleth map, first published in 1826. A choropleth map (sometimes called a cartogram – see chapter 21) is a diagrammatic map whose regions are variously coloured or shaded to illustrate a particular statistic, such as population density or voting choices. The first choropleth map designed by Dupin illustrated the illiteracy rate in France's regions.

A few years later, André-Michel Guerry (1802–1866) took Dupin's idea and began to build, embrace and extend. In 1833, he published his *Essay on moral statistics of France* which presented suicide and crime statistics in France on maps. The statistics were broken down and the maps coloured by just about every variable available. Guerry was fascinated by these charts and their social and economic impacts. He was the first to work in this field which later became known as moral statistics.

In 1854, a cholera epidemic swept through the city of London killing thousands of people every day. The health inspectors at the time believed that cholera was transmitted by infected air, but physician John Snow (1813–1858) believed that the outbreak was not airborne, but passed through the water supply. Using a map, he went door-to-door asking local residents about cholera deaths and marked each location to show the outbreak density. Using this data he traced the source of contamination to a local water pump and ordered the pump's handle removed, thereby preventing further spread of the disease in the neighbourhood. His map wasn't exactly a choropleth and it wasn't exactly a bar chart either. He mixed two chart methods to form a different kind of early visualization. Using geographically specific data, he concluded that the density of cases could be attributed to a local pump, strengthening his waterborne argument.

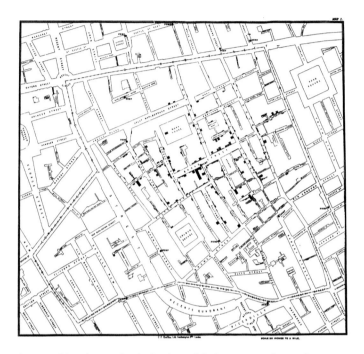

The next big advance in designing with data comes from Florence Nightingale (1820–1910). In 1858, while working as a nurse during the Crimean War, she emphasized the sanitary conditions in which the wounded patients were being treated. And there being multiple reasons why soldiers die while in hospital, she invented the polar area chart (see chapter 22), based on William Playfair's earlier pie charts from 1801. Her polar chart was a circular diagram of causes of death due to disease, wounds and preventable ailments. This illustrated the volume of lives that could have been saved given proper sanitary conditions: an early instance of hard statistical evidence being used to support changes in medical decisions and procedure.

In that same year, a French civil engineer named Charles Joseph Minard (1781–1870) pushed the boundaries of visualizations. He mixed multiple types of charts to convey more data and relationships. Taking a map of France, he overlaid several pie charts to show the geographic positions of the data sets. A few years later in 1869, he published his now famous chart depicting Napoleon's march into Russia. This has been hailed as one of the greatest landmark works in data visualization history. It is a flow graph which uses a map to show the relative transfers of goods and people, geographic positions over time and several other related pieces of data such as temperature and troop size.

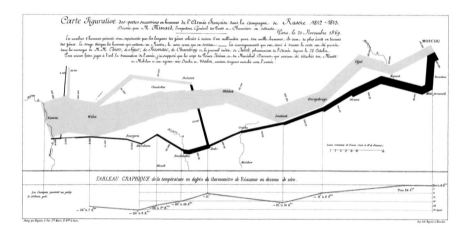

Within the last ten to twenty years, several new forms of charts have appeared. I attribute some of these to recent advances and innovations, but it's more likely that new charts and graph types are always being invented. Sometimes their usefulness is minimal and they disappear and no one remembers them. Only the recent developments that have not yet been proven useful or a burden seem innovative to us. Some of these new designs, such as treemaps (see chapter 18), will be discussed in this book because it is important to know their strengths and weaknesses before you jump in and use them in your own work.

2

CHART LITERACY

The amount of information rendered in a single financial graph is easily equivalent to thousands of words of text or a page-sized table of raw values. A graph illustrates so many characteristics of data in a much smaller space than any other means. Charts also allow us to tell a story in a quick and easy way that words cannot.

Graphs and charts are appearing more and more in our popular culture. Sites like Graph Jam[1] and Indexed[2] take concepts, song lyrics, observations and allegories and render them in rather silly or humorous pie and bar charts.

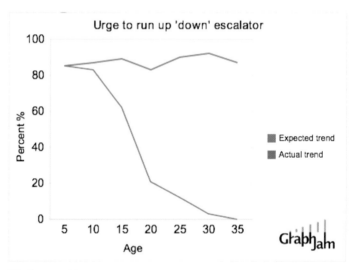

http://www.graphjam.com

We immediately understand them and they tell a story in their own right, sometimes more so than the original data. The fact that they give another dimension and life to the data demonstrates their worth.

Much of the value of graphs and charts comes from their clear, usable, legible interface whether on paper, screen or other medium. But graphs alone do not make something that is long, difficult and tedious instantly useful. It takes skill to be able to make a chart exciting and engaging without obscuring the facts.

---

[1]   graphjam.com

[2]   thisisindexed.com

Florence Nightingale used charts to improve the conditions for hospital patients and in the process saved countless lives. John Snow's cholera map transformed a table of dry names and addresses into a heat map of the affected areas. Both of these visualizations were clear and concise, and resulted in changes which benefited humanity. Had these been descriptions or raw values they would have been less likely to carry the weight that they had.

That's not to say that there aren't poorly designed charts or graphs that are useful. But this book offers five simple steps to creating effective charts and graphs by describing the situations where each chart type performs best and which to avoid completely.

And this is just the start of the journey: a well designed chart only gets you so far. Good graphic design is not a panacea for bad copy, poor layout or misleading statistics. If any one of these facets are feebly executed it reflects poorly on the work overall, and this includes bad graphs and charts.

Humans have been writing for thousands of years. The personal computer started the desktop publishing boom we have today (ten thousand fonts and all), and it was only very recently that charts and graphs became so easy to create, yet so often missing the mark.

With further explanations of the techniques of good design, we can improve the outlook for everyone, make the data clearer and tell a better story.

This book focuses on taking data and putting it into charts and graphs. Everything here is applicable to a fairly new term: 'visualizations'. It is a sort of empty word, simply meaning 'pretty pictures with statistical values'. I feel that, unfortunately, visualizations has become a buzzword. Several websites now list "the top 10 cool visualizations", or the "35 best visualizations of the year".

So what is the difference between a chart or graph and a visualization? My distinction is, perhaps, an arbitrary one and others will have different definitions, but a chart or graph is a clean and simple atomic piece; bar charts contain a short story about the data being presented. A visualization, on the other hand, seems to contain much more 'chart junk', with many sometimes complex graphics or several layers of charts and graphs. A visualization seems to be the super-set for all sorts of data-driven design. The fact that visualization has entered the vernacular reveals its growing popularity, even though no one seems to know exactly what it means.

Another indication of the importance of good chart design is the emergence of multiple awards, ceremonies and organizations championing and measuring chart design. All in all, chart literacy is an important tool, both for people creating the design to convey the message and for readers to understand the data's story.

3 Dynamic and static charts

With the invention of the personal computer came a much more interactive medium through which to view charts and adjust data values. In the past, charts and graphs were printed on paper and were as static as the medium. Both dynamic and static charts have their advantages and disadvantages. In this book, I will mostly address static charts and graphs, but the same concepts apply to interactive ones. Just because your design is interactive doesn't mean that you can throw away everything you've learnt about static chart design.

Interactive charts

The most common dynamic chart you are aware of is the weather map. When meteorologists give the five-day forecast and an animated storm front sweeps across the screen, this is a dynamic chart. It's displaying thousands of data points of storm intensity mapped on to latitude and longitude. When animated, it shows these values over time in a very complex way. It actually consists of several static charts rendered and animated to be played backwards and forwards. An animation saves a lot of space when compared with a printout of pages and pages of similar data. The downside is that only media that can play animations can use it.

That said, dynamic graphs aren't just animations. They can be designed to be interactive so that you can select only certain regions of the chart, or turn values on and off to remove clutter or focus on a subset of the items being tracked.

A well designed interactive chart allows the reader to manipulate the presentation of the data. A reader can zoom in to get a closer, fine-grained look, and zoom out to get an overview. Interactive graphs can isolate just a few aspects of the data and track them over time, possibly by adding a trail to the data to see where it has been in the past compared to the present.

For instance, in a financial line chart for all of the top 500 companies on the stock market, it should be possible to limit the data to those companies in which the reader owns shares. By making the chart interactive, you can reduce all the possible permutations that would need to be displayed so that the reader can have a chart of just the information required.

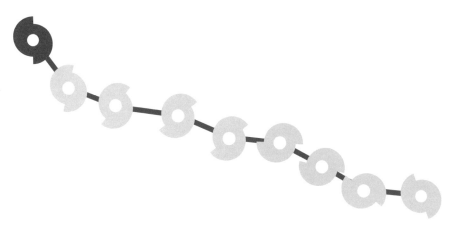

With animations, it might be useful to compare two non-sequential frames or leave a ghost trail. As the weather map follows the hurricane across the Atlantic, it could leave a small trail showing the path from start to finish. Many characteristics of data that are difficult or impossible to show in a static chart can be visualized using animation.

No matter if the chart is dynamic or static, the concepts in this book apply to both. The idea that the principles involved in selecting appropriate colours, chart types or white space are different for dynamic and static charts is incorrect.

My greatest concern about dynamic and interactive graphs is not how badly they can be designed, but about their longevity. We can look at the earliest extant charts and graphs from over two hundred years ago because they were encoded in an analog format; they were etched into metal plates and printed with ink onto paper. They were reproduced in several different books, magazines, newspapers and periodicals; no single source had the only copy of the design.

As we design fancy Flash® animations, MPEG videos, SMIL animations and use other proprietary formats that reside only on our one, fragile server, do we consider whether the files can be opened in two hundred years' time? The first computer-animated graph is probably already lost to us because it was rendered in a format now obsolete. This isn't a problem of lost back-ups or misplaced files, it is a genuine issue for forward-thinking design.

Animations are difficult in an analog world, but not impossible: an orrery is a mechanical model of our solar system. As the clockwork gears are wound, the planets move in relation to one another. Such a system doesn't suffer from file format incompatibility two hundred years after it was made. Can the same be said about some of the content that you are producing on a daily basis?

Dynamic graphs are excellent tools for exploring data, but if they can't be printed out or cast in metal, they won't last.

Static charts

Much of this book addresses static charts and graphs. I want to bring your attention to some of the benefits of them being static.

Analog formats last a long time. The Rosetta stone has an analog format: text cut into stone. It is several thousand years old and it works. The new Rosetta Project[1], which aims to record all the world's languages, has an online archive, but the data collected is also available on a micro-etched nickel alloy disc that can be read using a microscope. Static, analog formats such as paper

---

[1] http://rosettaproject.org

printouts, bound books and metal plates last much longer than digital files with specific encodings, file formats and digital rights management.

That's not to mention the versatility of static charts. When not constrained by animation, charts, graphs and visualizations can end up in the oddest of places. From newspapers and printouts, to statues and architecture.

Since there is no need for any mechanical or moving parts, static works can more easily be reproduced and shared in several different media, thereby reaching a much wider audience. This isn't to belittle interactive design, but it is a point to consider next time you get excited at the prospect of animating a chart just because you can.

4   DOES THIS MAKE ME LOOK FAT?

When designing any sort of visualization, you need to know how much space to allocate to the layout; this will determine your chart's dimensions. Depending on the content and type of your chart, the size will vary. Pie charts, radar plots and other circular charts need to be symmetrical, but others can be rectangular.

Then there are the qualities inherent to web and print. They are two very different media. On the web we can set text and container sizes as percentages relative to the browser window, whereas in print the paper has fixed dimensions. Each medium's strengths and weaknesses, as well as layout constraints, make designing charts for each medium different.

There is no correct answer as to what proportions are best, but here are a few pleasing suggestions and some details as to how our culture arrived at these dimensions.

Golden ratio

Phi or, as it is more commonly known, the golden ratio, has been a popular design tool for around 2,500 years. The ancient Greeks used this ratio in the construction of ideal buildings and statues. Notre Dame in Paris also has aspects of the golden ratio in its construction.

http://www.flickr.com/photos/bruchez/400273223/

The golden ratio is a specific ratio between two lines of unequal length. The ratio is golden when you get the same value dividing the smaller into the larger as you do when you divide the larger into the sum of both.

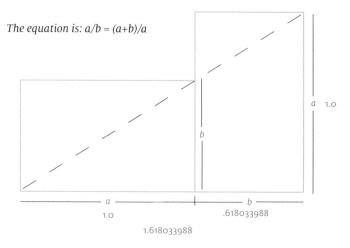

The equation is: a/b = (a+b)/a

This yields an irrational number. An irrational number is one that cannot be represented as a fraction of whole numbers. The golden ratio is often expressed as the value 1.618, but it is actually infinite. In ordinary use, this means that for every single unit of height, you need 1.618 units of width.

If mathematics isn't your thing and you have trouble remembering the decimal value of the golden ratio, there is a more straightforward system called the Fibonacci sequence.

Fibonacci sequence

Leonardo Pisano Bogollo (called Fibonacci after his father, Guglielmo Fibonacci) was an Italian mathematician who lived in in the late 1100s to early 1200s. He helped spread the use of the Arabic numeral system in Europe, the system we still use today. His other major contribution was his Book of Calculation (*Liber Abaci*) in which he discussed the Fibonacci sequence. He didn't invent the system, but popularized it such that it was named after him. The sequence has plenty of interesting uses in mathematics, but in this chapter we're interested only in the ratios.

The sequence of Fibonacci numbers is:
1, 1, 2, 3, 5, 8, 13, 21, 34 ... and it continues infinitely. The sequence is built by starting with 1 and adding 1 to it, giving the result 2. We then take that answer and add it to the previous value, in this case 1. 1 + 2 = 3. The process is repeated so that 2 + 3 = 5, 3 + 5 = 8 and so on:

$$1 + 1 = 2$$
$$1 + 2 = 3$$
$$2 + 3 = 5$$
$$3 + 5 = 8$$
$$5 + 8 = 13$$
$$8 + 13 = 21$$
$$13 + 21 = 34$$

The sequence isn't intrinsically interesting, but it's easy to remember. The useful part begins when you divide one Fibonacci number by the preceding Fibonacci number. Doing so results in an approximation of the golden ratio (1.618).

$$1 / 1 = 1$$
$$2 / 1 = 2$$
$$3 / 2 = 1.5$$
$$5 / 3 = 1.666$$
$$8 / 5 = 1.6$$
$$13 / 8 = 1.625$$
$$21 / 13 = 1.615$$

As the series continues the results get closer and closer to the precise value of the golden ratio. If you are looking for a nice rectangular ratio for your charts then select any multiples of two consecutive values in the sequence: 210 pixels by 130 pixels, 890 pixels by 550 pixels, and so on.

The golden ratio is similar to other common aspect ratios we see every day. The ratio 3:2 is used in 135 film cameras. The standard 35mm silver halide emulsion film is 36mm × 24mm. 3:2 is easy to remember and is close to the golden ratio.

Before widescreen (16:9) became popular, movies, computer monitors and television screens had a ratio of 4:3, which is somewhere between 3:2 and 5:3, but also gives pleasing results.

Using the Fibonacci sequence to derive a ratio is just one way to determine 'ideal' dimensions, but there are plenty of other equally valid, if perhaps arbitrary, choices.

ISO A series paper

A4 paper has an interesting ratio of $1:\sqrt{2}$ which is approximately 1.414. For each single vertical unit there are 1.414 horizontal units. An A0 sheet of paper has an area of one metre squared and each subsequent size has half the area. So A1 is half as big as A0, A2 half of A1, smaller and smaller each time, while retaining the same proportions.

1

1.41428571429

The advantage to the A series is that if you double the size of an A4 sheet, it fits exactly into an A3; if you have an A5 page, two will fit precisely side-by-side in an A4. All the ratios are perfectly tucked inside the next A series page.

This nesting makes for a convenient ratio when rotating, because the scaled version always splits the previous in half. From an A0 sheet of paper, all other sizes can be cut without waste.

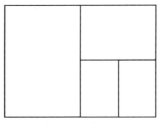

Nesting A series paper

16:9 Widescreen

The 16:9 ratio has been picked up as the widescreen format for movies and TV. It also has a ratio close to the golden ratio: 1:1.777 makes it slightly wider than 1.618 but still within the same general area and dimensions.

As more and more TV screens and films move to this ratio (though many movies use other, even wider ratios like 1.85:1 and 2.39:1), it might become more aesthetically pleasing in our culture. With 16:9 becoming the de facto standard, it makes you wonder, does art imitate life or life imitate art?

Silver ratio

If you have a golden ratio, then why not a silver, or even a bronze ratio? The silver ratio is another irrational number, a number that goes on and on, just like the golden ratio.

The silver ratio is calculated in a similar way to the golden ratio. You need two lines, one longer than the other. First, take the longer side, double its length and then add the shorter length. Then divide that total by the longer length. If the result equals the division of the short length by the long length, then you have a silver ratio.

a/b = (2a + b)/a

It all sounds quite complicated, but the final result is $1 + \sqrt{2}$, which gives a ratio of 1:2.414. For every single vertical unit there are 2.414 horizontal units. This makes a very wide (or tall) rectangle, even more so than 16:9.

There are several ways to arrive at a silver ratio. The easiest is to take a standard A4 piece of paper and remove the largest possible square from it. This has made its proportions a common size for compliment slips.

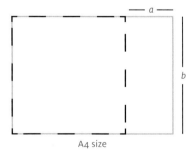

A4 size

What is left is a rectangle that is 1:2.414 in ratio. Now you can see the long and skinny aspect of the silver ratio.

Egyptian pyramids

The Greeks weren't the only ones with an ideal ratio. Before them, the Egyptians experimented with finding harmonies between two lengths. There is a great debate about whether the Egyptian pyramid builders used the mathematical concept of π (pi, 3.142) deliberately or that pi appeared naturally due to the use of wheels in construction. The circumference of circles can be calculated using pi (2πr). If an Egyptian builder paced out the length of a side of a pyramid as forty-two revolutions of his wheel, that distance is a multiple of pi. It is always possible, of course, that we have tried too hard to make pi fit into Egyptian calculations retrospectively – either that or it was aliens.

After the measurements of the Great Pyramid of Khufu (sometimes referred to as Cheops) were accurately determined, some experts asserted that the Egyptians must have been aware of pi. Before explaining what they based their claim on, we would do well to remember that errors in data don't always originate with the mathematics or visualizations, but instead at the source when the original data was first recorded (more on that in chapter 8). How is it possible to measure exactly the sides of a stone structure subject to 4,000 years of erosion? It isn't, but we'll humour those who made the effort.

If you double one side of the square base of the Great Pyramid and divide it by the pyramid's height, the result, approximately, is pi. There are plenty of conspiracy theories on why this is the case, so it must be said that all the pyramids have different heights and widths. The fact that the Great Pyramid's dimensions allow you to calculate pi is almost certainly down to coincidence or particular construction methods rather than a planned attempt at some perfect ratio.

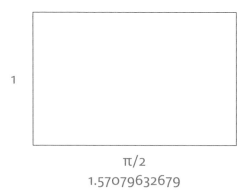

$$\pi/2$$
$$1.57079632679$$

Nonetheless, the result of pi/2 is 1.571, which is very similar to the 3:2 ratio we saw in the Fibonacci sequence and photographic film.

Other ratios

Anyone who studies vexillology (let's call them flag geeks) will know that the height to width ratios of international flags read like a number soup: 1:2, 3:4, 4:5, 6:7, 28:37, 21:40 and plenty of values in between. This might just go to show that every country feels that its flag deserves its own proportions – superior somehow to those of other nations – or, more likely, that there is no single ratio that is best for all designs.

Let's take all the ratios we've talked about so far and overlay them to see what they have in common. Most fall into roughly the same range.

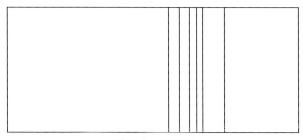

All stacked together

5 CHART JUNK

In his 1983 book, *The Visual Display of Quantitative Information*, Edward Tufte, an American statistician and information design expert, referred to all the pointless illustrations that go along with charts as junk. The definition of junk is wide and varied, but if you remove something from the chart and it doesn't change the meaning, it's chart junk.

We call it junk because it obscures the true meaning and intention of the graph, which is to convey information and tell a story. Any extraneous imagery is not part of the information. It uses up valuable pixels and takes short-term memory resources away from the data and draws the eye to the pretty pictures instead.

One example of chart junk is the use of imagery to form the bars in bar charts. Even companies that should know better give you the option to upload an image and use it in the chart.

	Label	Value
1	France	10,000
2	Sweden	30,000
3	USA	20,000
4	Poland	7,500

If you need to represent kilometres of railway track laid each year, then you might choose to draw a bar chart of the count. There is no need to style the bar chart to make the bars look like railway tracks or train carriages. At best it's cute; at worst it's unprofessional chart junk.

Chart junk isn't just misconceived graphics. It can be any unnecessary visual clutter. Adding pointless information and embellishments lessens the chart's ability to communicate.

This chart uses the common gender icons to illustrate how many more men or women visit particular websites. Can you spot the problem? (This example was taken from a real-world visualization.) Information is duplicated by the text value 52% and the additional two female icons. The problem here is that there should be four female icons. 100% – 52% is 48%: a difference of four per cent. The icons are not only misleading and wrong, but also unnecessary in this context.

When discussing gender differences, it is easy to slip into using the male and female icons seen on bathroom doors. If you find yourself doing this, ask yourself, "Can I delineate gender-related information without these icons? Is this chart junk?"

There are times when iconography is important. Gender icons are well-established across cultural boundaries. If your charts are to be produced in a local newspaper, text might suffice, but if the chart will appear in an academic journal being read worldwide by native speakers and non-native speakers, then icons could help remove ambiguity.

Junk in the trunk

Chart junk isn't limited to the chart data. When you begin to over- or underlay extra information like photos or graphs, it distracts the eye. We rarely put large amounts of complex text on to photos, so why put even more complex and dense data there instead?

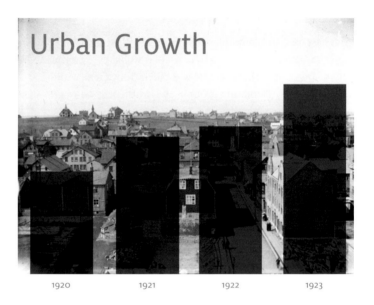

Keep your charts as free from clutter and open to white space as possible. The information needs room to breathe; don't throw more pointless data into the mix. The data to pixel ratio should be as close as possible to one (see chapter 6). Every pixel should be doing its best to be data, and tangential photos and imagery are designed to catch the eye rather than let the data tell a story.

Corporate branding

There is an old saying, "Do as I say, not as I do," which I think
is apt here. I'll be honest and say that I don't always follow my
own advice. And neither should you. We know that chart junk is
certainly junk, yet we sometimes add it in anyway.

I am guilty of this sometimes when it comes to corporate
branding. After spending hours of work crafting a cleanly designed
chart to explain very complex issues and being proud of my hard
work, I then put a giant watermark over the entire chart, just so
no one can claim it as theirs. You will surely have to make similar
decisions about this at some point in time: protecting the work at
the expense of legibility.

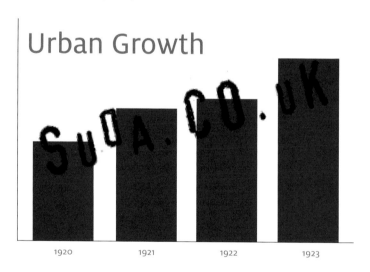

Some people are unscrupulous and will pass off another's hard
work as their own. A small logo in the margins of your chart might
get cropped out or erased, but a big watermark is hard to remove!
It is very tempting to do this and your client or boss might insist
on it. To me, a massive watermark over everything is rather like
peeing on it all to claim it as your own. It works, but there must be
a more elegant solution!

I also know that with computers the ability to mash up previously unconnected data sets to produce interesting results is easier than ever. In doing so, much of the layout is pre-built and the data flows into it like water into a bucket. Sometimes the data is messy, sometimes it isn't. Creating charts automatically with an application leaves less room for design decisions, such as where to place the logo. Because of this, on many occasions branding is faded into the background and is as large as possible so no matter the data, at least part of it can be seen. This might be a trade off you are willing to accept: your readers puzzle over what is in the background and you get the chance to have some branding visible some of the time.

This is also a way for companies to re-sell their charting software: your graph carries the manufacturer's brand unless you pay the premium to remove it or replace it with your own.

Ultimately, a balance must be struck between protecting the chart from plagiarists and not distracting or annoying your readers. A fine line, indeed.

Summary

Now that we know the perils of bad design, we're going to dig into the specifics of colour and ink. Getting the dimensions correct is important, as is keeping the chart junk out, but how do you achieve this? In part 2, we'll get into the specifics of highlighting specific portions of the design, how to use colour and ink to your advantage and, more importantly, how to use them correctly. Plus, we'll look at a few colour psychology experiments and potential hazards of not designing with tritanopia (a form of colour-blindness) in mind.

Part 2

Colour and ink

There is no denying the impact that colour has on us. Colour stirs
emotions, moves us to be patriotic, soothes our anger, builds
associations with specific products and warns us of danger. But colour
can easily be misused: too many colours and we can't make heads or
tails of the information; too similar a colour and we can't discern
a difference.

Traditionally, colour was made using ground up pigments, but
now on the web we paint freely with pixels. The range of colours far
exceeds anything we've had before. With graphics cards able to display
true colour in over 16.7 million distinct values, we are in danger of
overloading our readers. With ink, each new colour adds cost; with
pixels, it's a different story.

Data to pixel ratio

How to draw attention to the data

Rasterization ain't got those curves

Just a splash of colour

In Rainbows

6 DATA TO PIXEL RATIO

From Elements of Style, by Strunk and White

> "*Vigorous writing is concise. A sentence should contain no unnecessary words, a paragraph no unnecessary sentences, for the same reason that a drawing should have no unnecessary lines and a machine no unnecessary parts. This requires not that the writer make all his sentences short, or that he avoid all detail and treat his subjects only in outline, but that every word tell.*"

In his book *The Visual Display of Quantitative Information*, Edward Tufte uses the phrase "data–ink ratio" to mean the amount of ink representing the data divided by the total ink on the graph. This creates a ratio of data presented to total ink used, the idea being to minimize the amount of ink used on stuff that isn't adding value to the data. Don't be confused; the data–ink ratio is not advocating the use of as little ink as possible, but only as much ink as needed to convey the data. Just as when writing, you should write just what you need and nothing more, so too should you illustrate the data and nothing more.

A ratio of 1:1 means that every drop of ink used is data. This is hardly ever the case, so most charts and graphs have a data–ink ratio below 1:1. At the other extreme, a ratio of 0:1 means that none of the ink is conveying data.

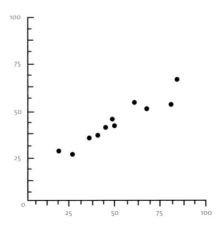

In this example, ink has been used to create the axes, labels, tickmarks and the data points. If we assume that the amount of ink used to draw the axes and tickmarks is 60% of the total ink, then we get the following ratio:

- data−ink ratio = (data ink)/(total ink used)
- data−ink ratio = 40 units/100 units

The data−ink ratio equals 2:3. More than half of the ink used to create the chart does not add any value. In this chapter we'll dig into how to reduce the unnecessary ink to level out this ratio as much as possible to 1:1. On screen, we're not dealing with ink. Instead, we can think of this value as a data to pixels ratio. How many unnecessary pixels were displayed to convey the message? Can we reduce that number and still say the same thing?

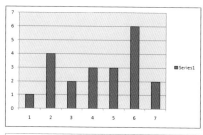

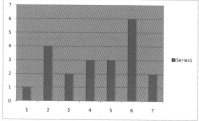

This is a standard chart generated by Excel. All the unnecessary pixels are highlighted. In a graphic that is 250px wide and 150px tall (37,500 pixels total) about 55% are lit up, all of them distracting your eyes and adding no value.

Had you asked someone in the year 2000 if it were possible to have conversations in bursts of less than 140 characters, they would have laughed at you; yet only a few years later SMS-length microblogging sites have sprung up all over the place. The constraint has been short messages: get to the point, rewrite and reword it until it fits. (Wouldn't it be great if e-mail were the same way! You gotta love senten.se[1]) We need to take a similar approach to designing with data. Cut out all the cruft and get to the story behind the data. Obviously the data points can't be removed so we need to focus on other information that we assume is needed and see if we can reduce those pixels.

The axes

Most graphs have an x-axis, a y-axis and some scale values. Some have grid lines to help the viewer. Much of this is superfluous and can be removed to increase our data to pixel ratio.

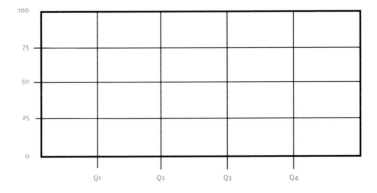

Once we begin to add the data, we can ask ourselves, "Do we still need all the grid information?" What if we start where the data starts and end where the data ends? That way only the data range is marked. This has two effects: first, it emphasizes the minimum and maximum values; and second, it reduces the number of pixels in the image. This technique can work on both axes.

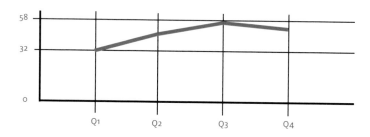

As you can see, by only labelling the data range, we can reduce the amount of pixels.

Remember, we still need to keep the baseline zero/zero scale. Later on in part 3, when we talk about how to deceive with data, we'll see why this is important.

Once we have set up the basic frame in which our data will flow, we can minimize its influence on the data. The story the data are telling us doesn't include the vertical and horizontal lines; it's the graph of data in between that interests the readers.

The axes, grid and labels should take the roles of a supporting cast and simply help the lead role when needed. By minimizing the line weight, lightening its colour, removing the portions not being used and reducing the labels, we can move the grid from the foreground to the background.

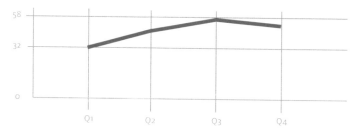

There's still room for improvement. On screen, it is hard to draw
lines thinner than one pixel; it is possible, but for these examples
we'll set one pixel as the baseline. When designing for print,
it might be possible to draw even finer lines.

We can go still further and remove those portions of the lines
that are above the maximum data value or below the minimum.
We can also remove the tick marks as separators.

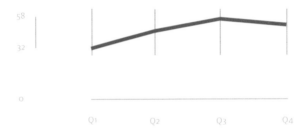

To retain the rhythm for each quarter, we can remove more parts
of the grid and the axis itself, leaving small lacunae where the
lines would have crossed the data line. Sometimes the absence of
ink can be as telling as the ink itself.

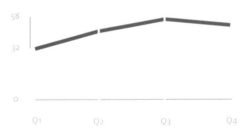

Here's another example where the frame has been reduced and gaps demarcate divisions which were previously shown with ink.

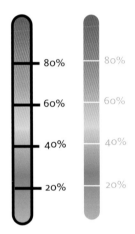

The goal is to reduce the amount of pixels needed for the chart overall, and this should start with the data frame. By keeping the frame to a minimum, you create an optimized place for the data, reducing the likelihood that it will go off course.

One problem with software packages is that graphs are generated with very few options to turn off or adjust the axes. For a professional chart or graph, you are forced to source or develop your own software to produce them properly. Using software to create charts quickly and easily is fine, but converting them to your own style can be laborious. Even so, it is worth the effort for the quality which can be achieved. Your personal approach to the data will be a breath of fresh air compared to the overused pedestrian designs of Excel, Google and other restrictive statistics software applications.

Any important document you produce should be proofread, spell-checked, edited and ideally professionally written. So why plonk an off-the-shelf graphic down next to it, and ruin all the hard work put into the text? It doesn't have to be that way.

Charts and graphs should have as much care put into their design as the text. They should complement each other, reinforce the company's brand and image as much as any other piece of photography or graphic design. Not only should the charts look good, but they should be formed properly and tell a story. This is the difference between a chart designed as eye-candy to fill space and a chart designed to show trends and hundreds of data points that would otherwise be an unwieldy table.

3-D graphs

Among the worst offenders that add pixels which contribute no additional value are 3-D charts.

Several off-the-shelf applications can make 3-D graphs and charts automatically, but at a huge cost to the reader. The legibility of your information soon becomes obscured by all the extra baggage needed to make it three-dimensional. Just look at how much space the pointless shadow takes up.

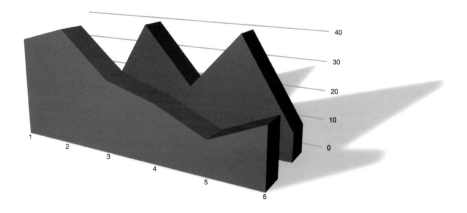

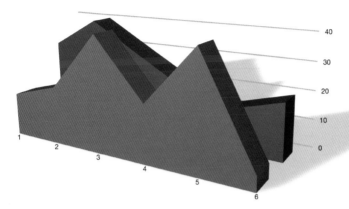

Placing lines behind other lines only works when the values in
the background are higher than those in the foreground – that is,
they're not hidden – but there is no guarantee that this will always
be the case. As you can see above, no matter the order of the data,
some part of it is invisible. The 3-D aspect of this chart does not
make the message clearer: on the contrary, it hides the facts.

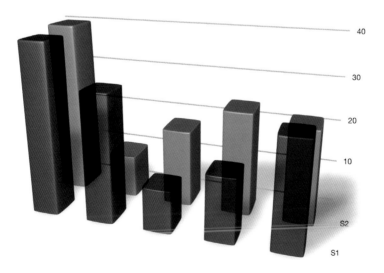

3-D line graphs make it difficult for the eye to determine the values in relation to the axes. And since they are offset from the baseline, it's difficult to compare data between two different rows of 3-D bars. Take, for instance, item 5 in S1: how large is that value? How does it compare to item 4 in S2?

Adding the extra pixels to create a 3-D chart doesn't add value; it simply adds more pixels and ink, reducing the white space and cluttering up the chart.

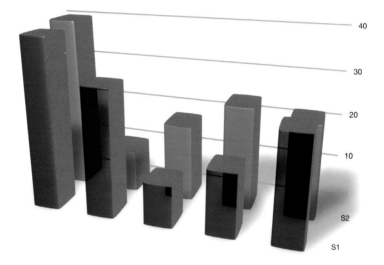

A large proportion of this graph consists of unnecessary pixels. Everything in pink could be removed without changing the story. In fact, it might actually improve it. How much of the reader's time has been wasted sorting out what is important and what isn't? In chapter 17 we'll go into more depth about bar charts and look at how to represent this same information in a more readable way.

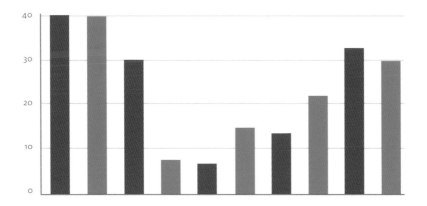

This is the same chart without the 3-D effects. It is so much easier to read.

A 3-D pie chart is probably the worst offender of all. It's important to compare the wedges from the same angle, but when we tip the circle all the data becomes warped because of perspective.

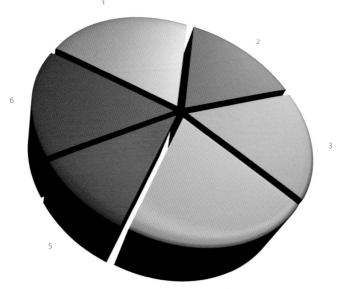

The three-dimensionality distorts the wedges: those closest to us appear to be bigger and the those further away appear smaller. Can you describe the percentage values for each wedge? Go ahead and try: the sum of the pie is 100%, so what are the individual values? As we'll see in chapter 19, which is all about pie charts, the only solution is to label each wedge and at that point you need to ask yourself whether the pie chart is redundant altogether.

If we look closely at the pie chart, you'll see that wedge 1 at top right is receding into the distance, so its perspective makes it look smaller. Wedge 4 at the front is made to look closer, so it is distorted further and the depth of the pie is visible, adding more pixels. In fact, wedges 1 and 4 are identical in value, but you'd never know that because of the perspective. Some people use this to their advantage to obscure the truth, as we'll see in chapter 19.

The whole point of a chart or graph is to clarify a jumble of numbers in a table. When charts are put into three dimensions, they do anything but!

7 ## HOW TO DRAW ATTENTION TO THE DATA

When tracking and plotting several different data sets, we often need to highlight some portions of data. There are several ways to call out specific parts of a diagram without drastically increasing the pixels required. What follows is a selection of ideas to do this. It is not an exhaustive list, nor will it work for every type of graph, but each draws attention and focus to particular parts of the data.

Colour

Colour is a powerful tool in highlighting information. There are two ways to use colour which make a particular item stand out.

Using a single colour within a black and white bar graph calls attention to that information without the need for extra labels. The addition of a single colour is a signal to the reader that something is different, but this works most effectively when that colour can have some meaning. When each piece of the chart is a different colour, then the impact of any individual colour is lost. This technique works when the graph is black and white, or a single hue. A sudden burst of colour demands attention.

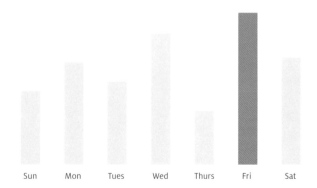

If the chart is already using a fixed hue, then it is possible to vary the intensity. Maybe this is only a black and white printout, or you are limited to a single corporate colour, but by scaling the brightness, contrast, lightness or transparency up or down, you can amplify or mute the information for the reader.

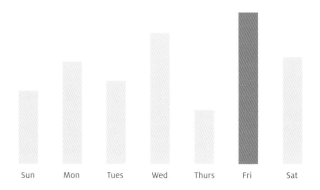

The lower the brightness, the darker it looks and the more it stands out. If the other bars are lighter they will fall away into the background; they remain visible for comparison if needed, but the main value has focus.

Weight

Another way to emphasize specific data is to increase its pixel width. On a line graph it is easy to change the thickness of each line to make them clearer, no matter the type of printer, or we can call out just one value and make it thicker so it stands out from the rest.

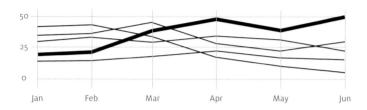

A brief warning: changing an item's weight might indicate something other than straightforward emphasis. For instance, changing the thickness of a bar in a bar chart could be misleading; perhaps the larger dimensions of the bar signify a stronger correlation with other data. We don't want to confuse the reader – we want to better tell the story. Altering the weight of objects could change the story in an unintentional way.

It is important to change the weight of a variable only when it won't be mistaken for another factor.

Position

The human mind is very good at creating artificial groupings based on relative position and shape. One way to provoke this tendency is through deliberate use of white space. Using white space effectively is more of an art than a science. I am sure there are heuristic equations somewhere that attempt to quantify this, but sometimes it is better to just go with your gut.

The position of some data relative to other data can lend emphasis. For example, take a list of quarterly returns on a bar chart. With some extra space between the fourth and first quarters of two distinct years, a natural association and grouping emerges.

Q1   Q2   Q3   Q4   Q1   Q2   Q3   Q4

It is also possible to isolate individual values and focus on them. If we had an average for all quarters in 2009, followed by the quarterly breakdown for 2010, we could push the average column away slightly so it remains clear.

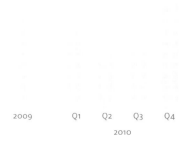

2009   Q1   Q2   Q3   Q4

2010

We've managed to isolate and call attention to specific data
or groups of data without having to add extra pixels to box in
information. A little more white space and proximity has done
the trick.

Shapes

Shapes offer an alternative to colour when identifying data sets.
Shapes have the advantage of working well in black and white, and
are therefore more robust.

You're probably familiar with the selection of horrible shapes
produced by graphing software when using multiple trend lines:
small squares, circles, triangles, crosses and others. While they
might not be aesthetically pleasing, they do play an important role
in distinguishing the data sets.

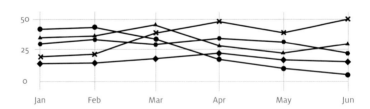

Take the scatter plot below. There are two variables, one on the
x-axis, the other on the y-axis. We can plot several different items
into this space, but we need a way to identify them. Colour works,
but can cause problems for readers with vision problems as we'll
see in chapter 9. Shapes are a good substitute.

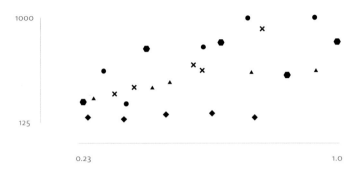

1000

125

0.23   1.0

A quick aside: many of the issues under discussion here are relevant beyond just charts and graphs. They can arise within interface design generally. Buried in Apple's iChat® program is the option to display the online/away status as shapes. For the small percentage of people who are red-green colour-blind, they can now make a distinction between the different statuses using these shapes.

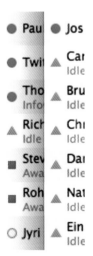

The downside with shapes is that there is a limited set of distinct shapes that can be used before they start to look too similar to one another. Circles, squares, triangles, crosses and stars are common; beyond that, the differences between the shapes become difficult to see, particularly at small sizes. The last thing you want is someone counting the sides of the shape to determine if it is a pentagon, hexagon or octagon.

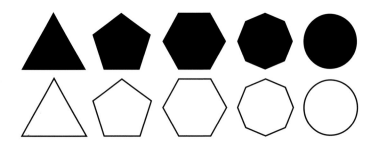

It is possible to use themed items, such as male/female icons, weather-related shapes and others but, as we have seen in chapter 5, this soon borders on chart junk and should be avoided.

Animation

With dynamic charts, another option is open to us: the ability to animate the data. With this power comes great responsibility, as an over-animated chart could look like a circus or pinball machine with movement and flashing lights everywhere.

Colour can be animated with a pulse or glow to grab attention. This was the premise behind the 'Yellow Fade' technique developed by 37Signals back in 2004[1]. When an area of the data changes, it is briefly shaded yellow before fading away and not constantly nagging the user. It says, "Yeah, I changed what you asked me to, and here's the result. If you need anything else, just ask. See ya."

[1] http://37signals.com/svn/archives/000558.php

Different weights can be applied in a static chart, but in an interactive world the user's actions can trigger the effect. Hovering over a line or bar can cause a change in weight or colour, or any other appropriate attribute. A reader's action could make the corresponding line brighter and thicker, and mute all the others.

Changing the position of a chart element in a static graph can be enhanced by movement. The item could rotate and spin, bounce or move back and forth, or go through some other animation. The problem is that the chart has the potential to become very busy.

Finally, shapes can be animated. Instead of a circle, square or triangle, you could add a spinning triangle or a pulsating triangle-square morph. This very quickly becomes pointless chart junk and falls apart when the animation is disabled, but you can see that it is possible to achieve additional emphasis through the use of animations.

Dynamic charts raise all kinds of questions. What happens when the chart is printed out? Is it possible for the reader to still distinguish the differences in the data? The animation was intended to make a distinction and draw attention to it but is the effect lost without it? Even if you intend the visualization to be seen only online, the reader always has the option of printing it out. When the medium changes, does the message change?

8   RASTERIZATION AIN'T GOT THOSE CURVES

An obvious problem with charting software is that it is designed almost exclusively for the screen. Programs like Excel, Google Charts and other paid and free alternatives all focus on output for the monitor. They often assume that what you are generating will be used in slideshows and stay only within the computer. We need to consider print media such as newspapers and books.

Your desktop monitor has a resolution of between 72 and 96 pixels per inch. In contrast, your local newspaper is printed at 150–220 dots per inch and most books even higher, at 300 or more. This means a good coffee table book is around four times denser per unit of printing than a computer screen, yet badly pixelated graphics are often transferred from screens directly into printed media.

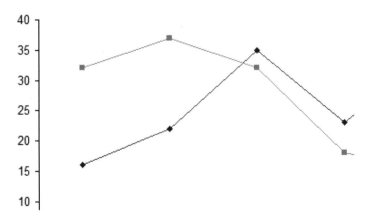

I have seen screenshots from Excel printed in newspapers. Due to scaling, one centimetre on screen and one centimetre in print are of very different quality. They take up the same physical dimensions, but the number of pixels in each is vastly different. Because of this, graphs look a lot more pixelated in print than on screen.

With all this horrible scaling a curve isn't smooth anymore, it's a jagged, blocky line. The reader's attention focuses on the poor quality of the visualization rather than on the data it tries to convey.

The higher the resolution of the printer, the more data per inch we can achieve. So why do we use the exact same charts in print as on screen? You end up with sloppy, pixelated printed graphs if you do not adjust.

If you are serious about your visualizations, then use a vector format rather than a rasterized GIF, JPG or PNG, not simply for the quality but to ease the editing process. If your final design is a rasterized graphic and then you are asked to change the text colour, unless you have the original or are some Photoshop® wizard, this is almost impossible to get right. Vector-based art allows for easier changes, even if the original file isn't available.

Vector formats scale nicely no matter the print resolution or size. Now, if you don't have an application that generates graphs in vector format, you can always trace them. This can be a tedious process, but the resulting quality is much higher and more professional.

As your workflow evolves, there are many possibilities as charts and graphs are generated programatically; for instance, a new weather map can be rendered and saved every hour. There are several formats you could choose from. As we've discussed, some obvious ones are GIF, JPG and PNG, but they suffer from the rasterization problem. In HTML5, we now have a new `<canvas>` element. It is a sort of sneaky halfway house between rasterization and vector. On screen it is a vector: you describe it as arcs and lines which are easily scalable, and it is then rendered to the screen. If your charts and graphs are only for this medium, then `<canvas>` works well, but as part of a larger workflow, the `<canvas>` element is rendered as a GIF and is not suitable for sending to a professional printer.

Another scriptable, vector-based solution is scalable vector graphics (SVG). You can view SVG in most modern browsers, and many vector applications such as Illustrator® [1] will open and save SVG files. Just as `<canvas>` describes the shapes as arcs and lines, so too does SVG, but in an XML format. Since SVG is a pure vector-based format, when printed at high resolutions it holds a much better curve. From a workflow perspective, this is worth considering. Do you create everything as SVG and then rasterize it as needed for each medium? Do you use `<canvas>` and target the dots per inch for different printers when rasterizing? By now, you'll realize that rendering as a GIF or PNG won't cut it, unless you have a large file size in height and width so that when it is converted from 72dpi screen resolution to 300dpi print resolution readers won't notice.

Have a look at any magazine or newspaper with a large readership and you'll see charts and graphs redrawn in a smooth vector format. In smaller regional papers, you'll more often see badly drawn charts (even the professionals aren't immune to this). This is usually due to the lack of tools, time or know-how to make it work in print.

If you are sending graphics to print, find out what the desired output size is. Applications such as Photoshop can adjust the dots per inch and you can make the rasterized version of your charts and graphs large enough so that in higher density printouts they won't be as prone to pixelation. It is best if you can design or trace your graphs as vectors, so you don't have to worry about various media or sizes now or in the future.

---

[1] See Illustrator and Inkscape: http://www.inkscape.org (free alternative available)

9 JUST A SPLASH OF COLOUR

Colour is a very powerful way to draw attention to specific portions of the design. Colour evokes feelings and emotions, making it an essential component in branding. There is a visceral response to and association between certain colours and brands. (T-Mobile carefully guards its hot pink in the mobile sector and what would Coca-Cola be without its red?)

On the web, we tend not to think about the cost of colour; whether we use one colour or ten, pixels always come for free. In offset printing this isn't true! In the movement from black and white to spot colour, to four colours or more, each time another process is begun, another ink, all adding cost. This physical process just isn't present when designing on and for the screen. Adding more colours into a print design raises the cost and that's the kicker. When you are designing charts and graphs that will be sent to third parties, it costs them to print, and we're not just talking about printing in colour. I've seen (and probably been responsible for) horrible oversights in this area! Airline boarding passes and other printable tickets that are so over-designed and branded that they use up a good chunk of the colour ink in my printer. And had I printed in greyscale, it would have just used a hearty portion of my black ink instead!

Henry Ford once said, "Any customer can have a car painted any colour that he wants so long as it is black". Although the Model T was available in multiple colours at various points during its production, there was a time when black was the customer's only option. This was due to a switch in the manufacturing process to a quick-drying paint that only came in black. It just goes to show that everyone is concerned about their ink (or paint) supplies.

With graphs and charts, we should take into account that each new colour introduced costs someone money. Knowing this, we also need to make sure that our visualizations work for the lowest common denominator: poor quality black and white inkjet printers. The information needs to convey the same story with or without colour.

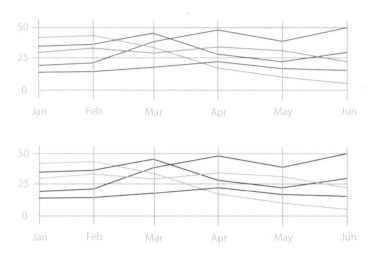

We've all seen ugly faxes that are so poor in quality that they are hard to read. Now, imagine that is your data. Is it so dependent on colour and print quality that it would just become a blob?

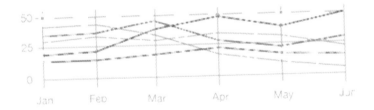

How can we avoid this and make sure our message gets through? Well, instead of depending on colour to convey the meaning, we can look into other aspects such as line style or thickness. All the things discussed in chapter 7 apply. Establishing a robust design will prevent problems in the future.

"But my design isn't for print, it's dynamic and will only ever be used on screen."

That's fine, but there are still several aspects that need to be considered, such as the distinct variations in the colours that can be used. Eight per cent of males suffer from some sort of colour-blindness. So when you say, "The red line represents annual growth", they can't identify the correct line; they see two greyish lines which are all but indistinguishable.

In colour or black and white, instead of refering to "the red line" you can change the thickness or add shapes. All the different steps discussed in chapter 7 are relevant.

Types of colour-blindness

Let's start out with a rainbow gradient consisting of all the colours in the visible spectrum. For people with full colour vision, this is the baseline which we'll render as if through various types of colour-blindness and compare the differences.

In one variety of colour-blindness it would look like the following:

Deuteranopia affects about five per cent of males, who are unable to detect medium wavelength colours. This makes it difficult to distinguish colour differences in the red-yellow-green portion of the spectrum and the indigo-violet end of the spectrum. If you have normal colour vision, the first half of the spectrum appears mainly in yellow tones and the second half lacks the red tint which combines with blue to make up purple.

Protanopia
effects ~ 1% of all males

Protanopia affects about one per cent of males. It has many of the same attributes as deuteranopia, but rather than medium wavelength detection problems, it is longer wavelengths that are missed. This results in a greater absence of the red end of the spectrum, making colours there seem even darker.

Tritanopia
effects ~ 1% of all males

Tritanopia affects less than one per cent of the combined male and female population. In this case the yellows are missing, making colours within the green to blue part of the spectrum indistinguishable.

If you use colour to delineate certain parts of your design, then you should realize that some colour-blind users might misinterpret your data. In the world of fashion, someone might confuse a red shirt for a green one and be mildly embarrassed. On the road, however, you don't want someone confusing a red traffic light with a green. To minimize potential accidents, traffic lights are always laid out red/yellow/green from top to bottom or left to right. A colour-blind person can at least rely on the consistent positioning.

There are several colour-blindness simulators online which can be used to view images as if through the eyes of people with the various types of colour-blindness. There is also a desktop application called Color Oracle'. which converts a whole computer screen into these different modes. This makes checking your design straightforward. Another benefit of running Color Oracle locally is that it can be used without sending potentially sensitive data over the web.

To help colour-blind people determine which colour is which, an organization called Color Add² has started a campaign to define a set of icons to represent all the primary and secondary colours.

The pictorial language starts by representing the three primary colours plus black and white.

Blue   Red   Yellow   Black   White

Using the primary colours, it's then possible to combine the shapes to make the secondary colours.

¹ http://colororacle.cartography.ch/

² http://coloradd.net

Blue   Yellow   Green

Adding the symbols for white and black helps express the shading of colours.

Light   Dark
Green   Green

It's a long way from describing the 16.7 million possible colours on computer screens, but for a limited set of hues it represents an alternative. And it is certainly an interesting project with some potential to replace those outlandish descriptive labels on the box of crayons or coloured pencils that we all grew up with.

For more information, you can read more at the Color Add website[1] and learn how to make greys and metallics.

---

[1] http://coloradd.net/codigo%20EN.htm

Colour quartiles

Using colour, it's possible to increase the density of information even further. A single colour can be used to represent two variables simultaneously. The difficulty, however, is that there is a limited amount of information that can be packed into colour without confusion. As we'll see in chapter 20, a scatter plot is capable of distinguishing four variables: the two axes; the shape of the data point to describe its type; and its size to represent another variable. By adding a single colour, it is possible to add not only a fifth variable, but also a sixth.

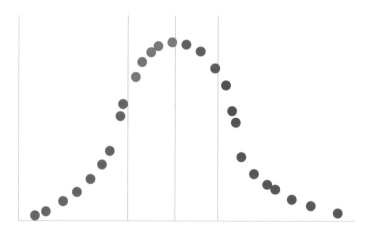

Let's say that we are measuring a school's national test results. Assuming a random sample, the results of all the schools will probably look like a bell curve. It is possble to break down that curve into quartiles: the values that separate the data into four equal parts. We could give each of those four parts a distinct colour, plot them and be done.

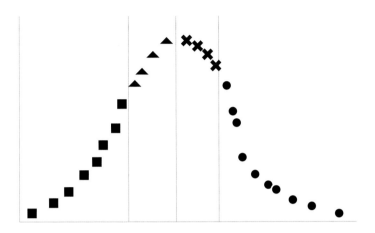

But what if we also wanted to measure a second variable, such as the students' happiness? Again assuming a random sample, there could be a second happiness bell curve with quartiles there too. When we graph these variables, we could use a second type of indicator such as a different shape or thickness. This would mean, for example, that we'd have some red (first quartile: test results) squares (first quartile: happiness) and all the combinations. Trying to include a third variable becomes very difficult and cluttered.

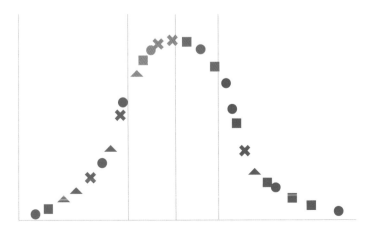

Instead, we could take the two existing variables and map them onto a 4×4 grid. This gives us sixteen possible colour combinations into which every school's test average and happiness must fall.

Happiness

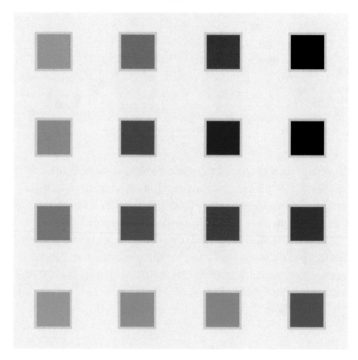

If we look at the example grid, the one:one box (top left) is a dark golden colour and four:four is a sky blue (bottom right). We could map the schools which have a very high test score combined with a very low happiness rating as one:four, the light green box (bottom left). Conversely, a school which has very happy students, but does not perform well on tests, would be a four:one, the black square (top right).

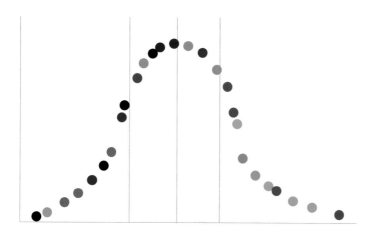

This is a very compact way to display data, as long as the colour distinctions are well defined and the number of colours is kept to a minimum. Here, we have effectively created sixteen buckets to put our data into. Now it is possible to use these sixteen colours in the illustrations and represent two variables at once.

 Downtown Primary School

Downtown Primary school has a blue colour which matches the four:four quartile. This school is in the bottom 25% in tests and bottom 25% in happiness.

 Middle Road School

Whereas Middle Road School is represented by the black colour: it tests in the lowest 25% percentile, but has a happiness rating in the top quartile.

Later a third variable could be encoded by changing the shape of the rectangular colour chip. Maybe the longer or taller it is, the more students there are in the school.

Stroop effect

In 1929, John Ridley Stroop, an American psychologist, published a paper about subjects' reaction time completing a task involving colour names printed in a different coloured ink. It's a very simple experiment to replicate.

What became known as the Stroop effect can be observed using some coloured markers, index cards and a group of friends. Write the names of colours on the index cards, but use a different colour ink than the colours' names: RED, BLUE, ORANGE, GREEN, PURPLE. When you flash up the word, the subject should respond as quickly as possible by saying what colour ink the text is written in, not the word itself. For instance, if the word RED written in green ink is flashed up, the participant should say "green", but their first thought will probably be "red", leading to a delay before their response, or an error. There are several online examples you can take to test your reaction time and experience the effect at first hand.

The Stroop effect reveals that the text (or, rather, the reader's comprehension of the text) has a stronger impact than the colour of ink used to print it. The issues of misdirection and assumptions are important factors in charts and design. As we'll see in part 3, it is possible to deceive with data because the brain focuses on different aspects of the representation, just as in the Stroop test we are primed for one response rather than another.

10 IN RAINBOWS

It should be obvious by now that colour plays a significant part in any visual presentation. Sometimes large sets of data are generated dynamically and you can't spend time selecting the perfect set of hues. What is needed is a way to choose a wide range of colours programatically and arrive at the same result every time.

The best way I have seen is a simple algorithm developed by Dopplr[1]. This takes a text string, in Dopplr's case a city name, runs it through some simple programming code and out pops a hexadecimal (hex) colour value suitable for the web.

For those of you who are not programmers, don't worry; there are plenty of websites which can do all of this for you. It just takes a bit of cutting and pasting on your part.

The algorithm is very simple and it isn't random, so you will get the same result for the same string every time. The first step is to apply an MD5 hash function to the text string. A hash is a one-way cryptographic function, but you don't need to know anything about cryptography to use this. The MD5 hash function converts any text into a 32-character hex string.

When we run 'Brian Suda' through an MD5 function it produces:

```
338c88ea7790424ec9ad2a3beaeab910
```

This value is, to all intents and purposes, unique. Every system that supports MD5 will produce the same answer, which is great because it's a consistent way of converting a string into a really big number.

A quick web search for "online md5" will find plenty of websites that take a text string and return a 32-character hex value. Try several different sites to check that the same result is returned each time – it will be. It is also worth noting that MD5 is case-sensitive. Typing 'Brian Suda' will give a different answer than typing 'brian suda'.

---

[1] http://blog.dopplr.com/2007/10/23/in-rainbows/

Now that we have our hex value of
`338c88ea7790424ec9ad2a3beaeab910`, how do we convert that into a
colour? The simplest way to make a six-character hex colour string
like those used in HTML out of the 32-character hex string we've
generated is to only look at the first six characters. In programming
parlance, we take a six-character substring. For non-programmers,
simply copy the first six characters of the MD5 result.

```
338c88 = substring("338c88ea7790424ec9ad2a3beaeab910",0,6)
```

The string 'Brian Suda' always equates to #338c88, which is a sort of
dark turquoise colour.

Brian Suda
#338c88

If you are working with applications that don't understand hex,
it can be converted into RGB values with a simple equation. To do
this, break the six-character string into three sets of two-character
hex strings: 33; 8c; and 88. Most drawing applications support
hex values, but it only requires a little bit of mathematics to
understand hex values and to convert them to decimal values
for RGB.

   Hexadecimal numbers use base-16. Base-16 means that instead
of 0–9, we have 0–F, where A equals 10, B equals 11, and so on up to
15. The hexadecimal value FF is (15 × 16) + 15 = 255 in base-10, our
normal way of counting. That's how we get #FFFFFF to be white
at RGB(255,255,255) and black #000000 to be RGB(0,0,0). For the
'Brian Suda' value, the hex number 33 is (3 × 16) + 3 = 51 in base-10.
So, 8c is (8 × 16) + 12 (140 in base-10), and 88 is (8 × 16) + 8 (136 in
base-10), giving RGB(51,140,136).

```
33    (3×base-16)+3
```

Using this MD5 technique means that the colours are reproducible across multiple machines, languages and instances. My name Brian Suda will be the same colour today as tomorrow on my computer or on another server. When using large sets of data, sets so large it isn't possible to sit down and assign every value a unique colour, using this alogrithm will save time and effort. To make this algorithm your own, you could just as easily take the last six characters, or the first, third, fifth, seventh, thirteenth or any combination. As long as you are consistent, you will get the same result time and time again.

The major disadvantage of using this method is that sometimes you get some ugly colours! Or white with off-white, or black with near-black. Or worse, several shades of the same colour that are very similar, making it difficult to distinguish between them. When such results are unavoidable, you need to make the best of a bad situation and adjust the layout and, perhaps, change the precision of the the data for the best visualization. For instance, if the month names create clashing colours, you can put the month and year name through the algorithm, for example, using the string "Jan 2010" rather than just "Jan", or "January" rather than the abbreviation. But remember to be consistent.

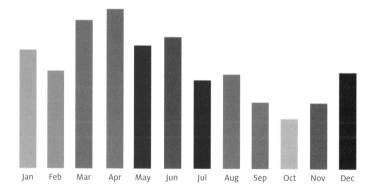

There is also a complementary algorithm which can help. It returns black or white based on a given hue. This equation is used to find whether black or white has more contrast with the colour. If the resulting colour is very light, this algorithm recommends using black text. If the colour is very dark, it recommends white text. It is a solution to the randomness of the MD5 algorithm when the value returned is unknown.

```
function contrast($hexcolor){
    return (hexdec($hexcolor) >0xffffff/2)? black : white ;
}
```

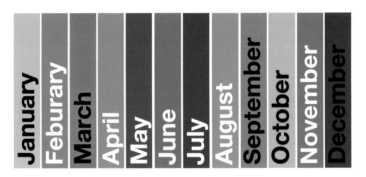

However, when you surrender completely to an algorithm you are stuck with it completely. Even if the colours are ugly and don't work, you must stick with it so it can be reproduced consistently.

One use for the MD5 algorithm is to generate background colours for a web page. This creates a little delight for your visitors, as each time they return to the site it can be a different colour. Like the BBC's homepage' which changes colour based on the colours in the main photo, you can use a random colour. Instead of using the source of an image as the colour we could use the current time on the server.

```
$backgroundColor = substring(md5(time()),0,6);
```

This will give a different background colour for every millisecond when someone visits the site. Again, you have to be willing to take the good with the bad, because there will be times you get hot pink, mustard yellow, mint green or a muddy brown.

Recently, I decided to change the face of my wall clock. Being inspired by the designs of others, I created a similar look, but wanted to generate the colours programmatically.

My first run produced horrible colours, so I changed the text slightly, but this didn't produce much better results. I realized that I can't change fate, so I went with the design as prescribed by the code. Through the algorithm I ran the text "00:00", "00:30", "01:00", "01:30", all the way up to "11:00" and "11:30", and saved the list of corresponding hex colours. The final design of the clock face is as follows; it's not bad, but not great, and I can always say that I didn't decide on the colours myself, so if you don't like it, you can't blame me.

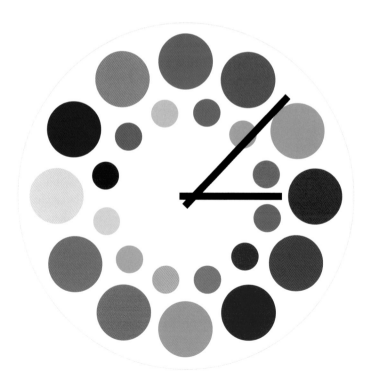

If your projects revolve around a large set of values that need to be shown in relation to one another, then this algorithm might be a useful tool for you.

Summary

Mixing and matching colours, removing lines until you can remove no more takes both a creative eye and the approach of a scientist who questions everything. The chapters in this section demonstrated the perils of bad chart design. Having poor quality graphics or too much noise both contribute to a bad experience. Designing with data needs to be about clarity in the story. Sometimes you need some characters to stand out and others to play a supporting role, but both are important in advancing the plot. Colour and ink are both used to achieve this.

As we've seen in this section, ink and colour are probably the largest contributors when designing charts and graphs, so you need to know how to wield them carefully.

As Antoine de Saint-Exupery, the author of *The Little Prince* said, "Perfection is achieved, not when there is nothing more to add, but when there is nothing left to take away." With practice, you'll reduce your data to pixel ratio to the minimum possible leaving only what is necessary for your readers to enjoy the story.

In the next section, I'll show you how to abuse what you've learnt to trick your readers into thinking something they shouldn't. I'm not showing you how to do this so you can befuddle your readers, but so that you don't get tricked. To outfox a fox, you need to think like one.

Part 3

How to deceive with data

"There are three kinds of lies: lies, damned lies, and statistics."
– Anonymous, popularized by Mark Twain

The impact of visualizations often tempts us to contort the data into the results we want. This is done both knowingly and unknowingly.

In this section, I'll run down a few of the different ways that visualizations can lie about the real data. It's important to understand these issues so you can spot bad design and avoid falling into these traps. In production, the chart might seem sensible, but if you know the pitfalls you can correct mistakes and avoid any misrepresentation.

Next time you read a newspaper or magazine, be conscious of the design decisions taken by the illustrator and wonder if they are deliberately trying to influence your opinion.

Trompe l'œil (trick the eye)

Relative versus absolute

Sins of omission

Caught red-handed: *The problem of false positives*

Fudge factor

(11) TROMPE L'ŒIL (TRICK THE EYE)

Human consciousness discerns patterns, even where none exist. Thoughout our evolution, predators have threatened to eat us and enemies attacked each other to take over territory. This sense of danger lies behind why our brains are wired to see shapes in clouds or cheese toasties. Our brains evolved to fill in the gaps.

We use this skill on a daily basis and it can be exploited for both good and bad. When presented with partial data, our brains try to find patterns and project the lines where data is missing which leads to misinterpretation.

Next time you wander down the main shopping street, have a look at the advertisements that span multiple shop windows. Does the ad stop at the window frame and continue again in the next pane leaving a few inches gap, or have a few inches of the advertisement been removed?

Hipposterous!

In chapter 6 we described the problems with 3-D charts and graphs, and in chapter 19 we'll talk about the problems people have judging the relative sizes of wedges in a pie chart. For now, we'll look at how readers assess the relative size of items of chart junk and other random or distracting shapes.

One way a chart can lie is through overemphasis of the size and scale of items, particularly when the dimension of depth isn't considered.

Let's take a simple bar chart comparing the amount of food consumed by two hippos. We see that Hippo One consumes two units of food, where as Hippo Two consumes four units. The bar chart correctly shows that Hippo Two eats twice as much as One because of the relative heights of the bars. This is as clean as possible, all unnecessary pixels have been removed from the chart.

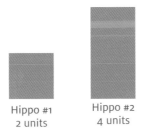

Hippo #1
2 units

Hippo #2
4 units

While this is an interesting statistic, maybe the illustrator wanted to show off a bit and try to make the chart more compelling by replacing the bars with sacks. It's a little kitsch, but as the chart is about units of food eaten, it's not a stretch to picture them as bags of food.

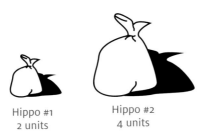

Hippo #1
2 units

Hippo #2
4 units

The scale still claims the same values: the first item is two units tall and the second item is four units tall. Nothing has changed in the chart except there are graphics rather than bars. The problem arises because we can all imagine actual bags of food in our minds and how much effort it will be to lift one!

The chart is disorienting because although it demonstrates a two-fold increase, the three-dimensional objects confuse our spacial awareness. Doubling the height of the sack effectively cubes the area, so the pixels used to draw the second sack represent eight times the amount, yet the illustrator passes this off as double.

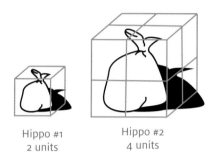

Hippo #1
2 units

Hippo #2
4 units

Even though we read the labels, our brain perceives the second sack as a lot more than twice the size of the first. If we were to take the 3-D nature of a bag of food into consideration, a doubling in volume would actually be represented like this:

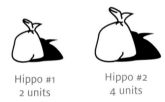

Hippo #1
2 units

Hippo #2
4 units

To the untrained eye, the second sack is barely bigger than the first. You'd be hard-pressed to guess it was double the volume, yet this is more or less what the values would look like in real life. The additional depth dimension makes the height appear much smaller than a doubling.

Turning this idea around, converting a competitor's sales figures into three dimensions can make them seem much closer to your own. If your competitors produce twice as many widgets as you, it's possible to hide most of the difference using depth to make you look less far behind.

Sometimes there is no connection between the size of the graphics and the values they represent. The scale of the second item is just made bigger and then labelled correctly. We are intended to believe the numbers, but the graphic makes a deeper impression on us and that is what we tend to remember.

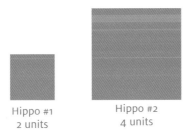

Hippo #1
2 units

Hippo #2
4 units

Even in two dimensions the visual representation can be out of scale. In the example above, the second item is drawn in a different scale to the first; it has been made arbitrarily larger. The numerical values might be correct, but the reader will remember only that item two is much larger than item one.

It is tempting to make charts more engaging by introducing fancy graphics or three dimensions so they leap off the page, but doing so obscures the real data and misleads people, intentionally or not.

When designing charts, it is important to avoid 3-D graphics which have an assumed volume.

The broken scale

Fooling people about the true meaning of the values doesn't end with graphics. It is possible to cheat with a broken or inconsistent scale. What would you think if you saw the following chart?

It looks quite dynamic, stretching from the bottom of the chart to the top. If the graph represented annual sales figures, then perhaps the company has shot up and is doing well. If it showed rises in the cost of living, we'd all be crying foul! What has been omitted is the rest of the graph below the data line. If that and a scale are added, the graph tells a very different story.

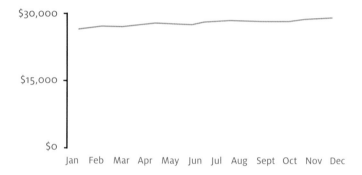

There isn't such a great movement when put into full context. The graph was exaggerated using a smaller, relative difference for a reason; it was designed to make an emotional impact. It wasn't about the data but the shape!

    This is why in chapter 6 we talked about not realigning the graph's origin. Even though our goal is to remove unnecessary pixels, we mustn't sacrifice understanding. Pixels can still be removed, but the scale must remain anchored and consistent.

Here, the unnecessary vertical tick marks have been removed so that only the minimum and maximum values are labelled, along with the origin so there is a consistent scale. There always needs to be a baseline for comparison, otherwise the chart is biased to the small, sample set of data being shown. Scales and context cannot be judged accurately without knowing the zero point.

The valueless scale

Another sneaky way to cheat is to create a graph with no explicit values. A line sloping upwards on a chart looks impressive but, if the scale is not provided, who is to say the steps are $1 or $1,000?

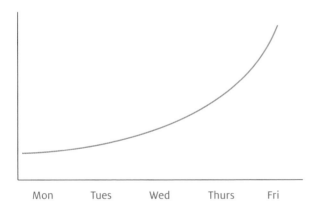

| Mon | Tues | Wed | Thurs | Fri |

Without any reference, we can't grasp if this is impressive or meagre growth. Given that labels were abandoned, Either the author is hiding the truth, or the entire chart was fabricated in an attempt to look significant without actually conveying any information at all.

By changing the scale, it is possible to change the shape of the
graph and, therefore, people's impression of the growth.

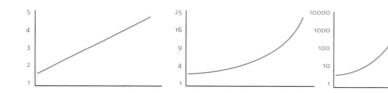

As you move from left to right, each chart seems to show ever
more impressive growth, but in reality they are the same chart.
In the first, the scale grows linearly: 1, 2, 3, 4, 5, and so on; in the
second, it increases polynomially: 1, 4, 9, 16, 25; and in the third,
logarithmically: 1, 10, 100, 1000. It is exactly the same data, but
plotted using different scales. This is why you should never trust a
chart that lacks some sort of explicit explanation of what is being
measured.

12   RELATIVE VERSUS ABSOLUTE

Another way to obscure the truth is to hide it with relative numbers. We're bombarded with this all the time in quotes like, "computer sales are up three per cent from last month". That sounds fine, but three per cent up from what?

Relative scales are always given as percentages or proportions. An increase or decrease of a given percentage only tells us part of the story, however. We are missing the anchoring of absolute values.

Take this truthful, but misleading press release:

> "ABC Widget Corporation had an incredible fourth quarter. It increased sales by 135% over the same time last year. If we compare that to its nearest rival, XYZ Cogs, which had only a 34% increase in sales this quarter, ABC Widget Corp. is flying high."

This looks like an increase of over 100% in sales for ABC Widget Corp. versus its rival. The problem is that this is only half the story. We are missing the absolute values.

A quick lesson in logarithms

A logarithmic series is one that increases by powers of ten at each step: 1, 10, 100, 1,000 on up; a zero is added to the end each time. So why is this important? Well, increasing ten widgets by one represents a ten per cent increase. Adding one to a hundred widgets is only a one per cent increase. One widget added to another one, and the widgets have doubled: a 100% increase!

Looking back at the sales figures for ABC Widget Corporation versus sales at XYZ Cogs, something similar is happening.

ABC Widget Corp. is a small, family-run business that sells around 10,000 widgets each quarter. In the fourth quarter, it happened to get a large order from a new customer and increased sales to 23,500, a relative increase of 135% and an absolute increase of 13,500.

XYZ Cogs is a multinational firm that sells around three million widgets per quarter. With a growing widget market, it added an additional 900,000 widgets in this quarter. That's only a relative 34% increase, but an absolute increase many times greater than ABC Widget Corp.

ANUAL GROWTH IN UNITS

ABC Widgets

XYZ Cogs

When we look at the numbers in absolute terms, then ABC Widget Corp.'s press release isn't as stunning as it originally sounded. With a production of 23,500 widgets in total, compared to XYZ Cogs' 3.9 million, it is laughable to compare itself to its rival in this way. The smaller 34% increase for XYZ Cogs is hundreds of times larger than all of ABC Widget Corporation's entire sales. The moral of the story is not to be fooled by relative values: they could be much less of a feat than the PR company would have you believe.

Using relative values to your advantage

There are times when you might want to use the relative values rather than the absolute. One example might be poll results. In my local free newspaper, there is usually some sort of survey question. I am very sceptical when the response values are 75% to 25%, or 67% to 33%. It just makes me think that only three or four people responded!

Relative values hide the number of participants (N), which can be a good thing in some cases. A poll that shows exactly the number of votes cast is an open invitation to spammers! If people can see that their individual vote has been added, some will keep voting to watch it roll over and over and over to the next number. With a very large N value, it takes many more submissions to move the relative values from 49% to 50% than to make an absolute count keep ticking over one higher each time.

In political elections, to show the N values might discourage people from voting in what is a close race relatively. If the tallies for the candidates were 51% to 49% with N values of 5.1 million to 4.9 million, voters might question the power of their vote and become apathetic.

Jumping lists

Another place where relative values are used without reference to their absolute positions is in lists. Shocking headlines that read, "More people worried about volcano eruptions than filing late taxes!" aren't really telling us anything. There is no reference point to understand how worried people are in these situations.

Imagine a list of life concerns. Maybe forgetting to file your taxes was 37th on the list and volcano eruptions ruining your holiday was 38th. In a particular month, perhaps more people worried about volcanic ash clouds and pushed it up to 36th place, forcing down killer bee attacks to 37th and pushing tax deadlines down to 38th place.

Simply saying that more people are worrying about volcanoes than tax deadlines is missing the point. The real question that needs answering is by how much.

This returns us to our lesson in logarithms. If a survey only found one person worrying about tax deadlines, then only two people need to worry about volcanoes to beat it. That's a 100% increase by doubling. But what if the survey found that 1,000 people were worrying about tax deadlines and only 501 about volcanoes? Again, a 100% relative increase would be needed to beat tax dealines, but now that means 500 people! When newspapers publish outlandish jumping list style headlines, you have to wonder if it was newsworthy in the first place. Omitting absolute figures for the lists is a pretty good give away.

13 SINS OF OMISSION

A sin of omission – leaving something out – is a strong one and not always recognized; it's hard to ask for something you don't know is missing. When looking into the data, even before it is graphed and charted, there is potential for abuse. Simply not having all the data or the correct data before telling your story can cause problems and unhappy endings.

Self-biasing surveys

There are surveys which eliminate some of the factors being researched. Phone polls work well for people who have phones! They also over-represent stay-at-home parents and retired people and under-represent the workforce, students and younger people.

> *"100% of the people we e-mailed use the Internet"*

A good survey organization will take this into account and either adjust the data accordingly, adjust the margin of error, or focus their polling on the under-represented groups in a different ways. But not all companies are so thorough.

The statistics are only as good as the cross section of data they represent. Asking 1,000 older people about their favourite video game does not make for a good survey result if you're trying to find out what will be the hottest this Christmas, even if scientifically conducted.

Missing data

Sometimes it is less about bad data and more about data that is missing altogether. In some situations, the group of people asked to participate is self-selecting; results can be biased because only those people available or willing to participate complete the survey.

I remember hearing a story that beginner's luck really does exist and that it disappears over time. I found it very hard to believe! Games of chance are just that, chance, not luck, and the longer you play, the more averages come in to force. It turns out that the explanation for the idea that beginner's luck really does exist is not mathematical but psychological.

Let's say ten friends get together to play a new card game. After the first game, five people lose; they are so disappointed that they quit and never want to play the card game again. The remaining five continue to play for the rest of their lives. The more they play, the more they feel that they had beginner's luck and as they lose (or, more accurately, the house catches up) it wears off. In some ways, for these players the myth of beginner's luck is true. In their eyes and the eyes of any observer, their record started off with a series of wins and steadily got worse. The missing data is all the people who lost in the beginning and never continued to play; they dropped out of the statistical pool. All of these people disprove the idea of beginner's luck, but they are nowhere to be seen.

The same goes for why all the places you visit seem more popular than expected. It is a strange phenomenon, but if we peel back the statistics we'll see it isn't so unusual. Is that favourite coffee shop always more crowded when you visit? Well, you are more likely to end up at a place when it is crowded than when it isn't simply because when places aren't crowded there are less people to make up the statistic.

Similarly, this is why it seems that our friends have more friends than we do. The probability that we will make friends with someone who has only one or two friends is very low, whereas the probability of making friends with someone who has a thousand friends is much higher. Therefore, it seems that your friends always have more friends than you do. You aren't considering all the people in the world with few friends that you don't know.

When looking at data sets produced by others, you need to ask yourself if there could be missing data.

Meta-analysis

If you throw enough information at the wall, something will stick. When searching for a specific result, you can run a test enough times to achieve any answer you are looking for. And if your desired outcome is a one-in-a-million chance, you just need to run a million tests.

It is like the infinite amount of monkeys typing on an infinite number of typewriters; one will eventually recreate the works of Shakespeare. Nothing is impossible, just improbable.

Within any given sample there will be outliers. If the sample set is small enough then these outliers can overwhelm the data. A company wanting to present itself in a particular manner can just continue to run test after test until the result it wants is achieved. This is how nine out of ten doctors end up recommending X as the leading brand. How many sets of ten doctors did this test include? Maybe during the first trial only three out of ten approved. Those results were trashed and the trial was rerun. Next time the results were worse and only one in ten approved. The tests continued until a set of nine doctors approved. At this point the tests were stopped and the company could slap a sticker on the product saying "Nine out of ten doctors recommend Brand X. It's been scientifically tested and approved!"

This is where meta-analysis comes into play. Meta-analysis consists of taking data from several trials and analysing them together as if they were from one test. The extreme outliers for the pros and cons will be smoothed into a more realistic reflection of the data.

CAUGHT RED-HANDED: *THE PROBLEM OF FALSE POSITIVES*

Just because the test results come back as positive doesn't mean that's the end of the story.

	True	False
Positive	True Positive	False Positive
Negative	True Negative	False Negative

When classifying data, there are four categories of results: true positives; false positives; true negatives; and false negatives. True positives and true negatives are easy to explain. Take, for instance, popular kebab meat, the kind seen rotating on spits. No animal ever looked like that: the meat has been processed. To test the meat to find out if it contains lamb, a sample is taken and sent off to the lab. A true positive means it was confirmed that, yes, this meat contains lamb. A true negative would confirm that, no, this meat does not contain lamb. This is pretty straightforward. Trickier and more error prone are false negatives and false positives.

A false positive is when something is reported as true when it is actually not the case. In our kebab example, the lab would report back that, yes, the meat contains lamb, when in fact it doesn't. A false negative is just the opposite, when the lab reports, no, this does not contain lamb when in fact it does.

Finding out what your dinner contains, however, might not be the most exciting example of false positives.

The same logic applies to every test that has some probability of an error – everything from carbon dating to DNA tests, Martian soil samples to loan agreements. With all of these examples, some cases are truly correct and incorrect, but others are always mislabelled one way or another. The key is to minimize or at least account for these situations.

Let's say you and your work colleagues are gearing up for a Subbuteo® championship. One hundred people enter the competition but, before it starts, everyone is required to take a drug test to check for performance enhancing substances. The test results are 90% accurate and take only a few minutes. To your misfortune, you have tested positive and are barred from competing. All those hours of training down the drain!

Let's assume that ten people really are taking controlled substances. After administering the test, nine out of those ten will get caught as true positives because the test is 90% accurate. This also means that there is one false negative: one person has slipped through the drug test net. He or she is taking controlled substances, but represents the 10% where the test failed.

So that leaves us with ninety honest, hard-working people. You'd assume that if they are clean, then they'll pass the test just fine. What's to worry about, right? On average, however, with ninety participants there will be nine people who are clean but test positive; a 90% accuracy rate for the test means 10% will test positive. In the sample set of ninety, there will be nine false positives.

90 Honest hard-working players

10 Actual cheaters

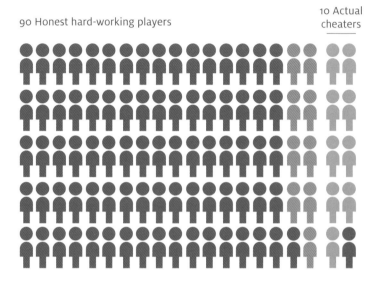

■ True negatives (people who passed the test and are clean)
▨ False positives (people who failed the test, but are actually clean)
■ True positives (people who failed the test and are taking controlled substances)
■ False negatives (people who passed the test, but are taking controlled substances)

So what are the odds that someone who tests positive is actually clean? Well, nine people have tested positive as false positives, but there were also nine others who tested as true positives. That means there are eighteen people who failed the test. So there's a fifty-fifty chance that any one of these people who have been removed from the tournament are not taking performance enhancing drugs.

Just because someone tests positive, doesn't necessarily mean that they are positive. Using a cheap test with a high margin of error will inadvertently flag some false positives. In this example, the sample group is small, only eighteen out of the hundred, and therefore longer, more expensive and complex tests can be used just on those eighteen to narrow down the positive results. Controlled substance tests, just like tests for cheating and money laundering, are screening for positive results. Therefore, it's best to minimize the chances of false negatives: someone who is actually cheating, but tests negative and slips through the net. In our sample set, there is one person who fits this category, the false negative. Mathematically, the more we reduce the chance of someone slipping through (false negatives), the more people accidentally get blamed (false positives).

The equation to determine false/true positives/negatives is pretty easy if you have the data.

If everyone in the US population, all 300 million people, were to take a free test which looked for a life-threatening disease, how many people's tests would be false positives? First, we need to know how accurate the test is; let's say that it is 99.9% correct in its diagnosis. Next, we need to know how many people are affected by this disease. In this example, only one in a million people.

To test how many people are safe from the disease (the true negative) we take the total one million and subtract the expected one to get 999,999 people who are expected to test negatively. We then divide that by the million to find the probability of not having the disease, which is 0.999. This leaves a very small chance that any individual is affected. Next, we need to take that probability and multiply it by our sample size (in this case, the population of the USA: 300 million) and then multiply the result by the accuracy of the test: 99.9% (or 99.9/100 = 0.999).

For our true negative count we'd have:

$$300,000,000 \times (999,999/1,000,000) \times 0.999 = 299,699,700$$

(population size) × (probability of not having the disease) × (quality of the test)

That's 299,699,700 people who test clean and are truly clean.

For our true positive count, we'd use almost the same equation, but instead of multiplying by the probability of being healthy, we use the likelihood of having the disease, in this case one in a million:

$$300,000,000 \times (1/1,000,000) \times 0.999 = 299.7$$

So just about 300 people will test positive and be positive for the disease – these are our true positives. This result also makes sense; if one in a million people have the disease, then we'd expect 300 people in our sample size to have it.

Now let's work out how many people are false positive. These are the ones who receive bad news when in fact they are perfectly healthy. This is the time when someone should ask for a second opinion or a different type of test to move them out of the false positive pool and into the true negatives.

We use the same equation as the true negative, except we use the probability that the test is wrong instead of correct, in this case 0.1% – the test is 99.9% accurate, remember.

$$300{,}000{,}000 \times (999{,}999/1{,}000{,}000) \times 0.001 = 299{,}999.7$$

It seems high, but makes sense if you understand that 0.1% of the people will fall through the testing margin of error. These 300,000 people are getting bad news, but are actually healthy.

But the worst category to be in is the false negative. You pass the test, but don't know you have the disease. We use the same equation as the true positive, but change the probability of the test to 0.1%.

$$300{,}000{,}000 \times (1/1{,}000{,}000) \times 0.001 = 0.3$$

Fortunately, there is less than one person out of 300 million who received a clean bill of health, but is very sick.

The false positives and false negatives are all the people who are at risk. In our case, 300,000 people were wrongly identified as positive and 0.3 people were wrongly identified as clean. That's one out of every thousand people who are incorrectly diagnosed. In a large population, that's a lot of people who could be told the wrong result even though the test is 99.9% correct!

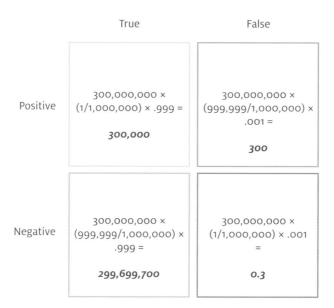

	True	False
Positive	300,000,000 × (1/1,000,000) × .999 = **300,000**	300,000,000 × (999,999/1,000,000) × .001 = **300**
Negative	300,000,000 × (999,999/1,000,000) × .999 = **299,699,700**	300,000,000 × (1/1,000,000) × .001 = **0.3**

To double-check that our calculations are correct, you can add up all the totals in each of the squares.

299,699,700 + 300 + 300,000 + 0 = 300,000,000

So every person in the sample set is accounted for in the matrix of possibilities.

However, the maths that makes the test 99.9% accurate through eliminating people as true negatives also means that a positive test result has a 99.9% probability of being wrong.

If we look at everyone who tested positive we get a total of 300,300. If someone received the bad news of a positive result, what are the odds that they are actually positive? To calculate those odds, we need to take the 300,000 false positives and divide that by all those who tested positive, whether truly or not: 300,300. That gives them a 99.9% chance of being clean even if they are given the bad news.

So the next time a doctor tells a patient that this test is 99.9% accurate and he or she has tested positive, the patient should know there is a 99.9% probability that the result is a false positive – I would ask for a second opinion.

False positives and false negatives are sometimes referred to as Type I and Type II errors. If you are interested in learning more, there is plenty of literature out there on this topic.

15 FUDGE FACTOR

One thing to be aware of both when designing visualizations and reading them, is the amount of information behind each data point.

A weather map gives a general impression of whether the temperature will be warm or cold, or if rain is likely. Somewhere along the line, someone thought about providing a three-day and then a five-day forecast. Forecasting involves taking advanced weather models and extrapolating out for a few days into the future, but the accuracy of past forecasts is rarely mentioned. Nor do people rely on the five-day forecast without checking again during those five days. There is a continual refinement of the information as time passes.

That said, what if you were planning a big party this weekend? If you consulted the five-day forecast on a Monday and there was a 60% chance of rain, what would the margin of error be? You simply don't know. If it were 60% plus or minus 30%, the possibility of rain would be anywhere within a 30% to 90% chance. Flipping a coin – heads it rains, tails it doesn't – has a better prediction accuracy: you have a 50% chance of getting it right. The forecast's margin of error is 60%!

The margin of error or 'fudge factor' is important, but it's something that is seldom mentioned or displayed.

One area in which margins of error are displayed is political polling. Organizations canvass people to ask if they are going to vote for Candidate A or Candidate B. It might be reported in the newspaper that Candidate A has a lead of 51% with a margin of error of 3%.

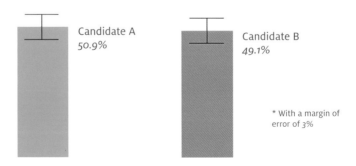

Candidate A
50.9%

Candidate B
49.1%

* With a margin of
error of 3%

With such a small margin of error, the difficulty is that in one poll Candidate A might be as low as 48% and Candidate B as high as 52% because three percentage points can be added or subtracted from each total. Claiming a victory for Candidate A when the margin of error does not exceed the difference between the two candidates' shares is a gamble at best.

Associated Press, taken by Byron Rollins

When dealing with statistics, there are several ways to generate a margin of error, but we need to worry less about the methods and more about the design of the data.

The most common way to visualize margin of error is whisker bars. Many software applications allow you to add these into your graphs and charts.

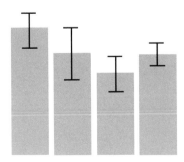

The whisker bars allow us to show a value at the height drawn, but provide a range within which the actual value might reside. These work well for discrete measurements, but in an example running over time, it might be better to have an upper bound line and a lower bound line. This gives an area in which the value could be recorded.

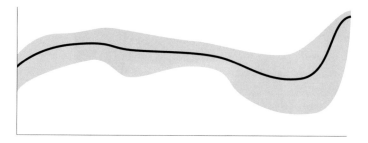

The line represents the recorded values, and the shaded area is the region where the values could appear given the margin of error at any particular time. The narrower the shaded area, the better. That means the measurements are more precise and the data will be closer to the measured value. In this example, the data could be at the very top or very bottom of the shaded region creating a large range of possibility for the true answer.

Certain types of data do not have margins of error. A budget assessment, for example, reports that $123.45 was spent this week or it wasn't. So area graphs, pie charts and others that can't have whisker bars are ideal for presenting this fixed type of data. Future projections, sample sets and experimental observations could well contain a range for each value which area graphs and pie charts cannot account for.

Precision error

An indication that the data is not statistically sound is when it is almost too precise. Saying that on average a family of four spends around $127.86 per week on groceries sounds much more scientific than saying that it spends around $130 a week. But where might such an exact value have come from?

It was probably the average taken from the sample. The problem is that nothing is known about the sample: was it 100 people, or 100,000 people? Were people asked to produce receipts or just write down what they thought they spent? Personally, I might be able to tell you how much I spent on my last trip to the grocery store, but for the last 52 weeks?

Be wary of any such exact values quoting the average anything of a group of people. One aspect we haven't discussed, which is beyond the scope of designing charts and graphs, is data collection. It is possible to create averages, graphs, time series and all sorts of fancy plots but if the initial data is not reliable then everything else that follows falls down. This goes back to chapter 13 about sins of omission.

There can be many issues surrounding the quality of a survey: the sample group and size; the self-selecting nature of the group, and so on. Asking people about their salaries rarely results in a precise average; people are often reluctant to reveal how little they make and tend to round up or, conversely, they might round down to put off the tax man, or even refuse to answer. Like the phone poll that reported that 100% of people have phones, there is always the chance of a built-in bias which charts and graphs cannot expose.

Confidence and error

The margin of error used in every calculation is related to the confidence interval. Since surveys only use a sample, say a thousand people rather than the entire population, it can never be said that the sample set exactly represents the true outcome. This is why a confidence interval is set; you are 99% confident, or 95% or 90% and so on. Lowering the confidence interval lowers the margin of error. If you are only 30% confident that the results are correct, then the margin of error does not have to be large. If you claim a higher confidence interval, then the margin of error also increases. It appears somewhat counter-intuitive, but that's the way it works.

The confidence interval determines the margin of error based on the t-value in a look-up table. There are whole textbooks written about sampling procedures, sampling error and confidence intervals based on the bell curve.

A quick note about averages

Something we all learned years ago in our mathematics lessons, but have probably forgotten, is that there are actually three different ways to reach an average: mode; median; and mean.

For the following values
1, 1, 2, 2, 2, 3, 3, 3, 3, 3, 3, 3, 4, 15, 121
we can compute three different types of average.

Mode
The mode is the most frequently occuring value in the set. In this example the mode is 3 because it appears seven times in the set.

Median
The median is the middle value in the ordered set. There are fifteen items in the list, so the eighth item is in the middle, separating the top half of the set from the bottom half of the set. The eighth value is 3.

Mean
The mean is what most people understand as the average. To calculate the mean, add up all the values, then divide by the total number of values. Thus, 169 divided by 15 equals 11.26.

From these results you can see it is possible to quote one average which is wildly different from another! An average of over eleven is impressive; an average of three less so. Neither is a lie: each one just reflects a selective use of the data to influence a decision.

Average personal income can be examined in this way. The salaries of the inhabitants of any given neighbourhood would yield different averages. One or two wealthy individuals could raise the mean because their high income gets spread amongst everyone else's. So when boasting about how great your neighbourhood is, you could inflate your status to the point where it makes you look the best. In this case, having a few wealthy individuals raising the mean makes you look good too.

The mode and median of the neighbourhood's salaries could be much lower than the mean. If everyone's salary was different, but maybe two or three people at the lower end all made minimum wage, then the minimum wage would be the mode and one possible average. But why would anyone want to quote their neighbourhood at the lower end? Well, maybe when it comes to paying council tax, residents could try to claim their area is poor and should pay a lower amount because the average citizen can't afford to pay more: the average person just makes minimum wage.

The same goes for the median – it too could be used to obscure the truth. It isn't a lie: the median value is an average, just not the expected mean average.

You should always fully explain which type of average you are using, and if you are looking at a chart that doesn't then you should be suspicious and ask questions.

Summary

I hope the next time you see an infographic, you'll look twice now to see if it is trying to trick you! Not everyone does it on purpose; ignorance of the issues is the most likely cause.

Knowing about these issues, you can always ask yourself how to redraw the chart to remove ambiguity. If you can dissect the design and rebuild it to be more understandable then you won't get fooled; plus, you'll learn how to create a better design if you run into the same problems.

So far we've spent the first three parts of the book learning indirectly about charts and graphs. We've delved into some background information and historical context, the problems of static and dynamic designs, and the physical dimensions of a chart. Then we moved on to ink and colour, learning how to set the framework for a good story, and how to call out and highlight specific portions of the data. In this section, we covered how people mislead with data design. Understanding this will prevent you from making the same mistakes when designing.

You've been given the groundwork for creating your own chart and graph designs. You have the knowledge to question what is wrong and the tools to fix mistakes.

In the next two parts, we're going to examine specific types of charts and graphs, pulling out a few common charts in Part 4 and discovering the situations in which to use each one. We'll weigh up the pros and cons, where each type of chart fails and succeeds, along with a bit of history and some things you probably didn't know.

In part 5, we'll spend five chapters looking at less common charts and graphs. There are two major reasons for taking time to study these more unusual forms. Firstly, when you do encounter these rare designs, you'll be able to spot problems with them. You won't be awed by something new and cool; you can sit back and say, "Sure, it's pretty, but it's not working well here." Secondly, as you graduate from the basics of charts and graphs and progress to visualizations and infomation graphics, knowing about the problems and failings of these more unusual types will be useful. They're not so common for a reason: they are either less effective, more difficult to interpret, or incredibly specific in their usage, all of which are important for a well-rounded designer of data to understand .

Part 4

Common types of charts

To speak any language, we start with the basics. This is no less true for the language of charts, graphs and visualizations. In this section, we'll discuss five common types of charts and the various ways they can be presented. It is important to examine the strengths and weaknesses inherit in each design; understanding the ins and outs of these common types of charts will help you identify the types of stories they are best at telling.

Line graphs

Bar charts

Area graphs and charts

Pie charts

Scatter plots

16   LINE GRAPHS

Line graphs are so called because they contain at least one continuous line which connects data points in a series. Multiple sets of data points can be plotted on to the same line graph. For instance, a line graph could represent time against income, or income against population; you name it, anything goes as long as there are just two variables.

Line graphs work best when the data is continuous. This could be a temperature rising and falling, the velocity of a moving object, or other continuous data. This type of data is information that can be sliced into smaller and smaller pieces and still offer a corresponding value.

This is where the line graph differs from other charts and graphs: its ability to tell a story between the plotted points – a story that is as powerful as the data that is known.

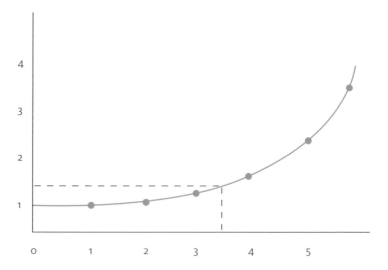

One of most common variables used in line graphs is time; we want to know how something is progressing through time. Time is continuous: it is possible to divide the units into smaller and smaller pieces. (Like that old story about talking a step halfway to the wall: you'll never actually get there – we can keep splitting a second into smaller and smaller pieces and never reach zero.) A line graph can also be used to project trends into the past or future. After the data points have been collected, a best fit line is created and extended in both directions. The validity of any projection is in no way guaranteed by the use of a line chart, but the chart can be used as a visual aid.

In the following table of dates and values, could you easily work out the point at which the company will break the one million dollar mark?

1 June	$200,000
1 July	$210,000
1 August	$220,000
1 September	$240,000
1 October	$290,000
1 November	$510,000
1 December	$780,000

What would you guess? January? Maybe February or March to be on the safe side?

What about if those same data points were converted into a line graph?

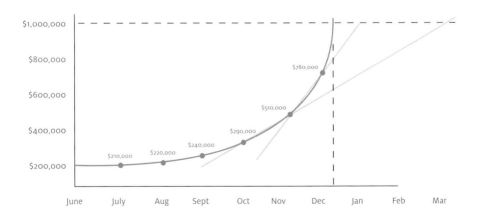

The line graph makes it much easier to determine the projected value at any point in time.

As well as displaying known points, a line graph allows us to look at the values between the points. Let's look back at our table. What was the value on 15 October, four and a half months into the data? On a line graph, we can draw a line up from the time axis halfway between the known October and November points until it meets the curved line joining the plotted values, and then draw another line across to the vertical axis to find the required value.

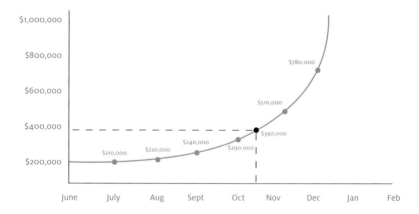

The answer is approximately $390,000; this is only an estimate, but it's probably a better estimate than just using the table would have generated. We can be pretty sure that the result is in the general area of that value.

Highlighting specific values

Chapter 7 demonstrated that there are several ways to use colour and shapes to distingush the different values on a line graph. We also saw how frugal we can be with the amount of pixels used in a line graph compared to other types of graph. Since line graphs are fundamental to designing with data, you need to always be aware of the strengths and weaknesses of how to bring specific values to the reader's attention.

Multi-variable line graphs

Creating charts that display one variable at a time is straightforward. Line graphs can track two variables with a single graph: one variable on the x-axis and one on the y-axis. But can we encode more than two?

It's possible to plot n dimensions, but this rapidly becomes confusing and enters into the realm of visualizations – the spectre of chart junk looms before us. It's a useful exercise to walk through how this happens and to see for yourself that the limits are stretched pretty quickly.

Let's take a company's net worth over time and plot those two on a line graph.

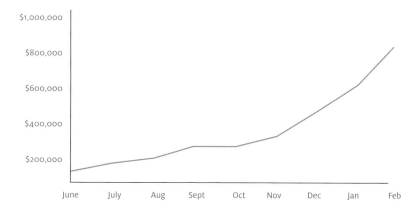

The longer the company is in business, the more money it makes. This is a standard two-variable plot: time and net worth. To add a third variable, let's map the number of employees into the line. The larger the dot at each measurement, the more employees work at the company. We'll be looking at problems with circles and relative size comparisons in chapter 19.

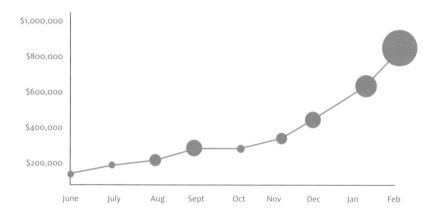

A fourth variable could also be illustrated by changing the colour of the line. Each colour might represent a different CEO.

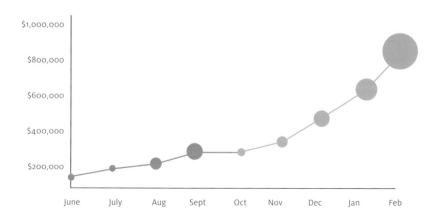

The number of variables that can be plotted is limited only by your imagination, the amount of colours you want to use and how far you take it before chart junk develops and the graph collapses under its own weight.

Sparklines

Sparklines are small lines introduced right into the text where the items are being discussed. Edward Tufte formulated this concept in his 2006 book, *Beautiful Evidence*, but it harks back to a much older idea. In the 1500s, Nicolaus Copernicus jotted down notes in the margins of his observation log books as he stared through his telescope at distant planets. Some of his notes took the form of small inline illustrations which acted like words. He was exploring such new territory in his studies of the heavens that he just drew pictures of what he saw rather than writing a lengthy explanation. Edward Tufte did something similar by embedding small line graphs within with text.

This week XYZ company's stock  shot up to 34th on the market

There are several computer applications which generate sparklines based on a data set.

The biggest difference between line graphs and sparklines is that a sparkline is compact with no grid lines. It isn't meant to give precise values; rather, it should be considered just like any other word in the sentence. Its general shape acts as another term and lends additional meaning in its context.

The driving forces behind these compact sparklines are speed and convenience. Instead of discussing a team's performance and then referring to "Table 3 on page 896", the information is displayed right there, inline. It keeps the reader in the flow of the text, adds information where it is needed, aids comprehension and gives a scale and weight to the values in the prose. If I said, "It was a great year for the company!" it might sound impressive; having a sparkline available would let people decide if my excitement was warranted or not.

17   BAR CHARTS

The bar chart is the go-to chart, the Swiss Army knife of charts – it can be your bread and butter. There are so many ways to take this basic idea and adapt it to make many other types of charts. You can decorate it with whiskers and candles, rotate it, add handles and bedeck it with all sorts of jewellery to further tell a story.

Unlike pie charts, as we'll see later, bar charts have the ability to easily display two variables, one on the horizontal axis and one on the vertical. Pie charts can show two variables as well, but one will always be a value relative to one hundred per cent. Bar charts can take this much further and more meaningfully.

The biggest benefit of bar charts is that different items of data can easily be compared visually. A horizontal line can be drawn from the axis or the top of one bar across all the others for easy comparison. When each bar is properly labelled, it is also possible to reorder the values without losing information – bar charts can be ordered from lowest to highest, alphabetically or any other way – as long as it best tells the story.

Bar charts can also employ many of the aspects we discussed in chapter 7 about highlighting specific data; colour, spacing, size, and so on, can all be changed to create new associations. Multiple items can be compared next to each other, such as male/female count by grade.

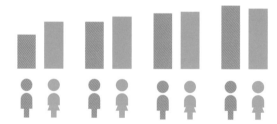

Line graphs versus bar charts

You might wonder how a bar chart differs from a line graph. There is no hard and fast rule about when to use a bar chart rather than a line graph. Each makes a few assumptions which, depending on the data, need to be considered. A line graph assumes that any point on the line is measurable and a value can be extracted. If the values on your horizontal axis are 1, 2, 3, 4 and so on, then every point on that line has a value. For instance, you could compute the value of the line for 1.5 or 3.14 or 5.618.

A bar chart models discrete values. There might not be a bar chart value for 1.5 unless there is actually a bar there. This is why there is normally a space between the bars of a bar chart, to show that they are not connected and that one value does not flow into the next. There are some instances where the bars can be put together, when the data does flow, and we'll discuss these histograms later in this chapter.

With bar charts, order is not necessarily important. Each bar is independent of the others, so they can be sorted alphabetically, by value or in some other order. With a line graph, the correct order is essential since the data represented is continuous.

What determines whether you should use a bar chart or line graph is the type of data and how flexible it is. The differences are subtle, but can be very important overall.

Whiskers

One advantage of the bar chart is that the bars can be decorated to reveal some additional statistical information. As we saw in chapter 15, there is often a fudge factor, a percentage that might be over- or underestimated. This is often seen in political polling: Candidate A is leading 54% to 46% with a margin of error of plus or minus 2%.

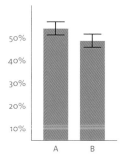

To illustrate this using a pie chart is impossible – there is no way to add this four per cent buffer – but with line and bar charts we can. Whiskers added to each bar reveal the upper and lower boundaries of the data.

Each whisker is a small vertical line representing plus or minus two per cent from the value, with some horizontal lines to make the ends easier to see and measure. As discussed in chapter 6, the data to pixel ratio should be kept to a minimum, so remember to keep the design as light as possible.

Taken to extremes, the bars are removed from the chart altogether. Rather than using all the ink for the bar, what if the value was shown as just a point? The whiskers can extend vertically from that.

Depending on your needs and how abstract you want this line of thinking to be, this reduction in ink can be taken quite far.

Candlestick chart

You might not have heard of a candlestick chart. It's a very specialized chart for financial data, but is basically a bar chart in disguise. Knowing how a candlestick chart works could be useful, because you might be asked to model some data which has similar characteristics and, rather than reinvent the wheel, you can use this bar chart derivation.

The candlestick chart was adopted around 1900 by Charles Dow, founder of Dow Jones & Company and *The Wall Street Journal*, and it has remained in the financial world ever since. Its origins actually go back to the eighteenth century Japanese rice market. However, it doesn't really matter how it started or where it came from – knowledge of how the design works is the important part.

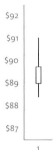

The bar in this case represents the opening and closing prices of the stock. Here, the stock on day one opened at $89.10 and increased in value to $89.80. So the bar portion starts at a little over 89 and continues just about up to 90. That's straightforward and not unexpected in a bar chart. The whiskers, or wicks, that extend up and down do not measure margin of error, but the maximum and minimum selling price on that day. On day one the lowest offer was not much lower than the opening price, whereas the highest value was $91.00, significantly higher than the $89.90 closing price. Perhaps at some point in the day some great news was released about the company, causing the price to rise. But later, traders discovered that the news wasn't all it was cracked up to be, so the price declined slightly back to around $90.

Day four in the following chart shows something very different. The opening value is $90.90, which follows from the previous day's closing, but the closing price for day four is $88.80, much lower than $90.90. To represent this loss, the bar is coloured in, either in black or any solid colour, whereas a gain is white or no colour.

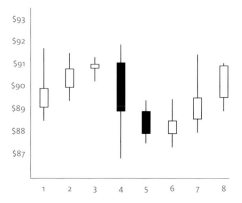

A candlestick chart provides an effective overview of the highs and lows within a given period of time. It won't describe every last detail of what happened between the highs and lows, or precisely when they occurred, but it does reveal a trend, something that would be near impossible in a table.

Financial traders give special names to the patterns that emerge from the different design possibilities: hammer; inverted hammer; spinning top; and others. It isn't important to know these names, but if you want to dig deeper into the history of candlestick charts and their jargon, there are plenty of resources online.

Histograms

Histograms have many of the same characteristics as bar charts, but they have some significant properties of their own which make them distinct.

A histogram represents frequency over a closed range. Grades on a test, for example, must lie between zero and one hundred per cent; every grade will fall along that line somewhere.

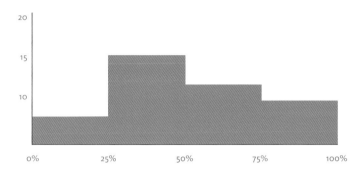

Let's put each grade into one of four buckets: 0–25%, 26–50%, 51–75% and 76–100%. The height of the bar is the number of grades in each bucket. This follows similar rules to bar charts except that in a histogram the correct order is essential. It doesn't make sense to place the 76–100% set first.

Histograms create an overall picture, quite often tending towards a bell curve shape; there are a few people in the lower groups, most in the middle, then trailing off again toward the high end. Since the data consists of ranges and flows from one container to the next, there are no gaps in the values and there are no gaps in the chart. The bars are placed right next to each other, sharing a vertical edge. Bar charts are illustrated with space between the bars, but in a histogram they touch.

Another aspect of histograms, also because of their range distribution, is that empty sets must be shown. The same sample data, spread across ten buckets rather than four, might reveal a completely different distribution.

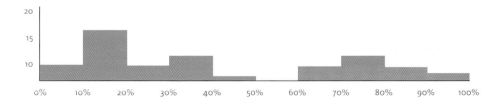

In this case, there were no grades between 51–60%. This could be omitted in a bar chart, but in a histogram it is important to retain and display the empty space. It contributes to the picture of the data as a whole.

When data is in a continuous range with a fixed lower and upper bound, a histogram is a useful way to present the information.

The return of chart junk

Be aware that bar charts provide ample opportunities for chart junk. The space within the bars is enticingly empty and it is tempting to put images or textures in the background. Some designers even swap out the standard bars for graphics. As discussed in chapter 5, this is a bad idea – it's chart junk, plain and simple. It adds no value to the data and distracts the reader from the real story.

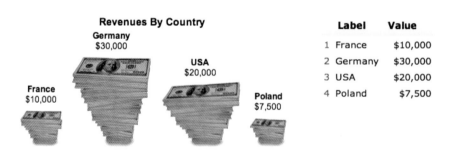

	Label	Value
1	France	$10,000
2	Germany	$30,000
3	USA	$20,000
4	Poland	$7,500

	Label	Value
1	France	10,000
2	Sweden	30,000
3	USA	20,000
4	Poland	7,500

Star ratings

The most famous star rating has to be the one found in the Michelin Guide in which restaurants are awarded one, two or three stars. There is much to criticize about the awarding process, but as a rating system it works well. So well in fact, that many other star rating systems have appeared, from five star ratings for books and movies, to hotel ratings systems. Even two thumbs up is a rating system.

But how is a star rating related to a bar chart? If we think about what a bar chart tells us, it has a maximum and minimum value defined by the axis. The bar then extends through the space and stops at the appropriate value. A star rating does something very similar; think of it as a horizontal bar chart. The minimum number of stars is zero and the maximum is either widely known, or is shown as empty stars. The value of the 'bar' is the number of visible stars or stars that have been filled in.

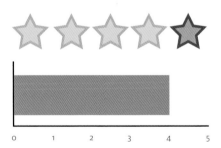

The equivalent bar chart can be reduced in pixels almost to match star ratings, but some things are implicit in star ratings that need to be made explicit in a bar chart: namely, the scale values. Star ratings rarely use anything besides whole and half stars, so it makes the steps easy, whereas a bar chart can take any value and therefore the step size must be displayed.

Star ratings also have the interesting quality of having fewer characters than their text equivalent. When there is a single rating value, it makes sense to simply display that. As we'll see in chapter

23 about gauges and thermometers, sometimes people feel it necessary to explain one value by wrapping it in a large amount of chart junk. If a movie received five stars, isn't it better to write "5 stars"? But that's seven characters, whereas the Unicode star (★) written five times is two characters less and tells the same story. That's something to think about when looking to reduce the data to pixel ratio.

In several Unicode fonts, there are characters for a filled star and an empty star. BLACK STAR (U+2605 ★) and WHITE STAR (U+2606 ☆) can be used instead of images in your text, HTML and documents. Not all fonts support these characters, but some of the pre-installed ones do, such as MS Gothic and MS Mincho on Windows and Apple Gothic on a Mac.

While star ratings have a limited range of use and are in danger of being overused (and they can also cause confusion – do only whole stars count or half stars as well? What's the maximum to use? Can your eleven star rating map to my two thumbs up system?), they are still a useful tool as long as you understand that they are just a particular visual representation of a bar chart.

(18)

AREA GRAPHS AND CHARTS

If you are dealing with multiple data sources and you want to see the data broken down by each item as well as the sum of all the parts, then area graphs are the solution. There are area equivalents of all our favourite charts, each providing both general totals and particular results. They come in various guises: from stacked bar charts and area graphs to area bar charts. In this chapter we'll take a look at some examples and how to use them.

Let's imagine three roadside stands: one selling lemonade; one selling hamburgers; and a third selling fresh vegetables. The stands are in place for the whole summer, a period of twelve weeks. Each week, the vendors calculate their sales figures, providing thirty-six data points to be plotted.

Since time is a factor, it makes most sense to plot time along the x-axis and label the twelve weeks of summer, and on the vertical axis to plot the three stands' sales figures. There are two ways to achieve this. The first is a series of bar charts next to each other. This follows everything we have learnt about bar charts and good design. The grid is minimized, three distinct colours are available, and the weeks are carefully spaced to make logical groups and reduce the total pixel count.

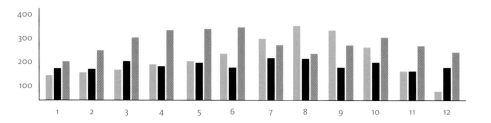

Depending on the story we are trying to tell, this might be the ideal representation. If you want to compare this year's lemonade income to last year's, or compare vegetable sales to hamburger sales in this summer period, bar charts in series work great.

Stacked bar charts

On the other hand, if you are more interested in seeing how
profitable this strip of highway is for roadside stands, you might
want to see the cumulative sales figures. To achieve this, the bars
from each chart are stacked on top of one another. This shows
not only the week with the greatest sales, but also which stand
contributed most to the total figure during any given week.

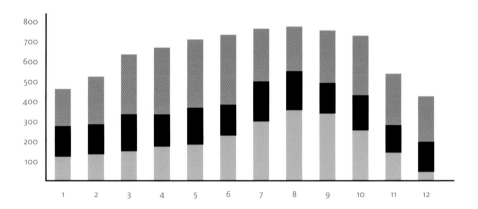

Stacked bar charts describe totals while allowing a degree of
internal breakdown of the data. In this example, the overall
income from the sales is illustrated well, but only the first stacked
values (blue) can be accurately compared as they share a common
baseline. The middle and third stacked values (black and orange)
never start at the same place, so it is harder to compare one weekly
value to another. The one advantage is that the order of the stack
can be swapped without changing the overall total.

Like regular bar charts, stacked bar charts can be illustrated
both vertically and horizontally. The orientation you choose
depends on the space available and the data being described. In our
example, sales are graphed over time. The convention is that time
is plotted horizontally, but if we were using a different variable,
such as location, then rotating the illustration so that location is

on the vertical y-axis and sales are plotted along the horizontal
x-axis is an acceptable design descision.

As we discussed in chapters 16 and 17 about line graphs
and bar charts, there are different situations when you might
choose one over the other. Line graphs show a continuous change
whereas bar charts represent a single point at a time. Since a bar
chart and a line graph demonstrate different attributes of the data,
the area equivalents of each also have particular purposes.

Area graphs

An area graph is usually a series of stacked line graphs. If we were
to take our roadside stand data and convert it from bar charts to a
series of line graphs, and then stack those to create an area graph,
we produce an effect similar to the stacked bar charts, in that total
sales over time can be seen.

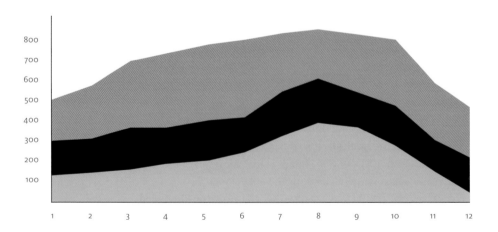

Area bar charts

Stacked bar charts take the existing data and stack it to reveal a
different perspective. Stacking the different bars creates something
equivalent to a pie chart. It visualizes the relative percentage
of each item in a particular week, but since the bars represent
absolute values rather than relative ones, we could keep
making these stacked bars for each week and compare them to
one another.

What if there was a way to get this relative view when the
values are stacked, but also encode a second variable? Since the
data sets are stacked, their shapes can't be changed to a star or
circle. But we can change the size in one dimension.

The stacked value for each week shows the total number of
units sold split into three sections. What if we also wanted to
display the profit margin? Selling 100 units of one product might
only make $1 profit on each one, whereas selling 50 units of
another product might generate $3 in profit each time for a total
of $150.

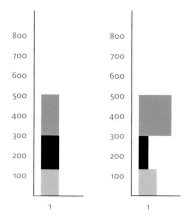

To represent this, each segment can be extruded as if it were a
horizontal bar chart – though we must be careful not to overload
the reader. Each axis must be carefully labelled and there's a
danger that the display of the full twelve weeks will be cluttered.

Still, it is possible to present multiple variables in a stacked bar chart – something that can't be done with an area graph. As soon as further variables are added to a stacked bar chart it becomes known as an area bar chart.

Those dotted pie chart wannabes

You know all those teenagers who rebel against conformity? Yeah, those same ones that all dress the same and conform to this nonconformist ideal. The same ones who, when you try to explain this to them, get all frustrated and walk away in a huff.

Well, this next kind of area graph is just a pie chart in disguise. It knew how bad pie charts really were (you'll see what I mean later) and didn't want to conform, so it went off and did its own thing, thereby conforming to something just as ineffective.

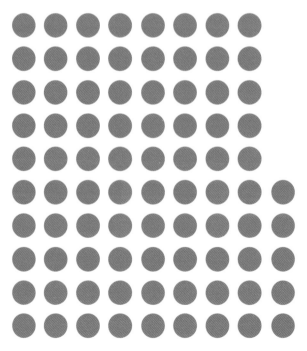

This is an attempt at an area graph, but broken down into small units, each representing a fixed number. Maybe each circle equals one or ten or maybe a million: it doesn't matter. The chart purports to show a percentage of a whole and an absolute count at the same time. Rather than make the data sets flow into a bar chart or line graph, the data is forced into odd shapes.

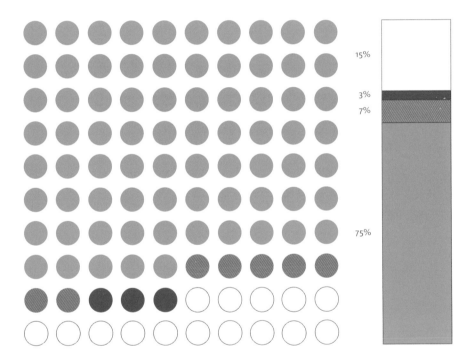

One advantage is that the dots are countable, but it also means that the upper bound needs to be included. If you want to represent 75%, 7% and 3% you need 100 dots, but only 85 will be coloured in. This helps to clarify that the dots represent percentage totals, otherwise they are just 75, 7 and 3 units. By omitting the upper bound, the chart is just a bar chart with kitchy chart junk.

Stream graphs

Stream graphs have emerged only recently. Their name stems from their appearance: a river or stream of data pouring down or across the graph. They have many of the attributes of an area graph, but don't display them particularly well.

The first was created by information designers Lee Byron and Martin Wattenberg in an example for last.fm in late 2006. A little over a year later, *The Washington Post* worked with Byron and Wattenberg to create a stream graph to display box office revenue[1]. The data produced a beautiful twisting ribbon of the ebbs and flows of a fickle public's movie-going habits.

When you create a stream graph from a data set, your mileage may vary. Here is some sample data which produces what looks like a psychedelic slug trail rather than aiding understanding of the data hidden within it.

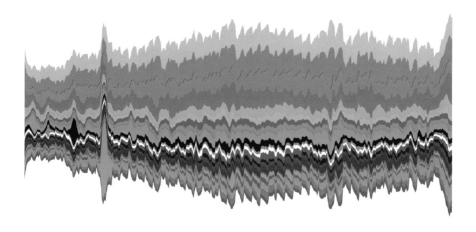

[1]   http://www.leebyron.com/else/streamgraph/

Instead of having a zero line, the stream graph bubbles out from the horizontal centre line. Where the stream goes below this line, it isn't showing negative values: the whole stream is simply realigned for that time period. Also, without a baseline, it is very hard to figure out the scale and distance to calculate the area delineated by the curves.

The graph below shows a slice of a thousand tweets from my Twitter stream broken down by word and visualized as a stream graph[1].

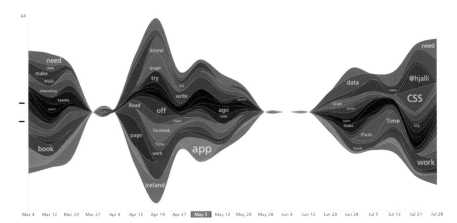

Your Twitter stream will appear quite different; the variety of words you use will affect how flowing and stream-like the design is. It's still not particularly readable or useful, but it is an example of an area graph and it's worth understanding its limitations before deciding to use one.

They create beautiful visualizations, a torrent of information all flowing together, but stream graphs don't convey the data as well as some alternatives. Any stream graph can be made into an area graph by setting up a fixed baseline, so the data only grows in one direction. The jury is still out on whether stream graphs will prove worthwhile or can find a niche.

[1]   http://www.neoformix.com/Projects/TwitterStreamGraphs/view.php

Treemap (mosaic graph)

A treemap is a relatively young chart type that has the ability to show multi-variable information using both relative size and colour. In 1990, Ben Shneiderman, a professor of computer science at the University of Maryland, experienced the common problem of running out of computer disk space. He wanted a way to visualize the entire disk and see how much space was taken up by each directory and subdirectory. To scratch this itch, Shneiderman required a new type of graph and he invented treemaps out of the necessity to better understand the data.
(He has written more about his experiences and the thought process on his website[1].) In my research for this book, I found a statistical atlas of the United States, published in 1870, which contains what looks like an early treemap.

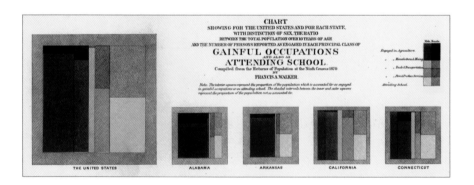

The concept, then, has been around for a long time and was rediscovered and refined only recently.

A treemap has a defined area, usually rectangular, which represents all of the data under examination. It's similar to a pie chart, but square. Each of the items being measured is allotted a relative size within the larger rectangle. No matter how many

---

[1] http://www.cs.umd.edu/hcil/treemap-history/index.shtml

smaller pieces are arranged inside, they can all fit within the larger rectangle. This yields a tiled view of all the items relative in size to each other. Given that they are also squares or rectangles, they are rather easier to compare than round shapes. It is still difficult, however, to compare lots of smaller values.

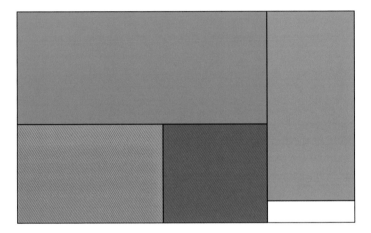

The advantage of a treemap is that you have plenty of boxes which can contain information about a second variable. A good example of this might be a book store. It can start with all the relevant sections: history; politics; cooking; travel, and so on. The whole box represents the total sales in a given quarter and each smaller box within corresponds to one of these genres. We can quickly see which have been the biggest sellers during that quarter, but we still have the ability to layer on one more variable. In this case, it makes sense to colour code the rectangles based on the rate of change. If a box is shaded green, sales have increased since last quarter; if it is red, sales have decreased. Of course, it is possible that everything could be green, because sales could be up across the board! So, we'll have to think carefully about colour.

A treemap, much like a geographical map, can't express changes over time unless multiple treemaps are used, or some kind of animation moves from one treemap to the next.

In the interactive world, a treemap made up of categories of books
could be activated by the user, and then the selected category
becomes the full treemap and all the subcategories can be mapped
within it. Each of these in turn can be activated, revealing further
subcategories or individual books. Because each box in a treemap
is itself a small treemap, it is possible to drill down further and
further in a dynamic fashion.

A treemap may or may not be suitable for the data. Since a
treemap describes all of a data set, a pie chart could be used (we'll
see in chapter 19 if this is a good idea). A stacked bar chart might
also be an option; this shows all of the data in a consistent width
bar for easy comparison, but if there are many items the bar chart
might extend a long way in just one direction. A treemap tends to
make all the areas within it square and therefore more compact. It
is not always possible, however, to show different parts of the data
in similar dimensions. This forces the reader to compare two areas
across the distance of the treemap which are drawn at dissimilar
ratios and sizes (the same applies to wedges of a pie chart).

One way to solve this is with the stacked bar chart, since the
dimensions for each item would be similar, but it doesn't solve
the issue of comparing two items over a large distance. The other
problem with a stacked bar chart is that the ability to display a
second variable represented by a different colour is lost. Putting
two bars next to each other with the same colour would make
them look as if they have merged into one; a unique colour for
each item represented is needed. For a small number of items this
is feasible, but a treemap excels at representing large volumes of
data and we know from chapter 9 that colour can be problematic.

Another potential way to respresent the data is a standard bar chart. Each item would have its own bar of similar dimensions and, because they are distinct, the second variable of colour could be kept and comparing or reordering the bars accordingly is straightforward. The advantage of the treemap over a bar chart is that it saves space and similar items can be clustered together, but comparison and labelling suffer in exchange for compactness.

Horizon graph

Horizon graphs are a kind of overlaid line graph. They are a relatively new invention, so their usefulness is still undetermined, and their strengths and weaknesses are still emerging. They were developed by a data visualization company called Panopticon to better visualize and compare several data sets over time, side by side without overlapping them.

In our roadside stand example there are three separate businesses, but what if there were thirty? Thirty bar charts per week lined up next to each other would be too much. A stacked bar chart gives us the total sales, but what if we wanted to compare within each week? We could make a line graph for each store and then plot all thirty on the same graph. That, too, would quickly get overcrowded with information. As we've seen, once we exceed about five or six, we start to run out of unique colours, shapes, thicknesses and so on. Graphing thirty at once becomes a mess.

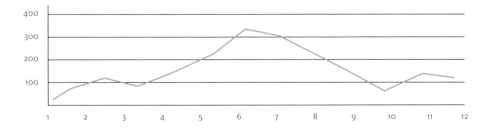

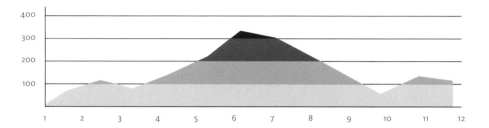

This is the niche that horizon graphs are designed to fill. They are basic line graphs split horizontally into a set number of bands. This example uses four bands, but they can contain as many as required. Each of the bands is coloured with an increasing intensity of blue. So far, this is no different than a standard line graph with some interesting shading.

    The next part is the Eureka! moment. Since we are really only interested in the outer edge of the line graph, why not collapse each of the bands on top of each other to save space?

Now we have the same data presented in a quarter of the space. By changing the colour of the shading, the graph appears to be stacking up the parts. There is nothing hiding behind any of the peaks so, unlike 3-D charts, nothing is being obscured.

    This works with both positive and negative values. Maybe in some weeks the shops were making a loss, which can be represented with a different colour, such as varying intensities of red.

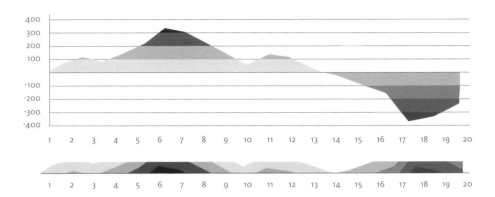

Now you can rapidly see which weeks saw gains and which saw losses, and at the same time also watch the line trend upwards or downwards.

The horizon graph works really well when large numbers of data sets need to be compared. Converting one line graph into a horizon graph does save some space, but now that we have this ribbon, we can stack more ribbons on top to get a quick view of all the different shops and compare them in a limited space.

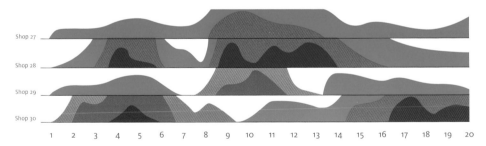

The downside of horizon graphs appears when the data sets are very large. This example was broken down into only four colour bands; this was sufficient to allow each to be distinct. The more bands required, however, the more colours and the greater potential for confusion. By limiting the number of divisions, each band represents a larger portion of the data. To compare several horizon graphs, their coloured bands need to represent the same divisions; if they don't, the comparison will be difficult.

19

Pie charts

I won't hide the fact that I am not a fan of pie charts. They are the scourge of the graph and charts world! They add little or no value over a table of figures and can easily be misused to misrepresent the data.

Even popular culture has latched on to their ridiculousness. Sites like Graph Jam[1] and Indexed[2] are constantly making jokes using pie charts.

One of the problems with pie charts is that the amount of data they represent is very limited. The total value of the information must add up to one hundred per cent and therefore a pie chart can only represent relative amounts. If you remember, in chapter 12 we discussed the issues of relative data: comparing data across sets is problematic because ten per cent of one data set can be a vastly different absolute amount than ten per cent in another.

The most effective pie charts comprise only two items, such as the percentage of male or female customers. If we introduce more than two wedges, the eye must rotate at least one of the wedges to a cardinal point to figure out the percentage value. With only two wedges the angle is shared, making it easier to determine the proportions of each.

If one side of the wedge follows a cardinal direction, then only the arm of the angle which doesn't needs to be compared. When the two values meet at the 12 o'clock position, only the bottom half needs to be examined to see how much more or less each value is compared to the other. If the segments do not meet at a cardinal

[1]   graphjam.com

[2]   thisisindexed.com

point, then it is more difficult to calculate the angle and estimate the values. The reader is forced to rotate the chart so that one line is perpendicular and then work out the angle.

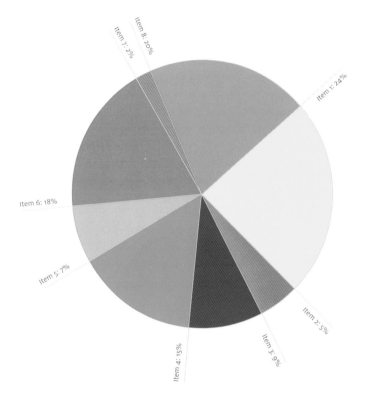

As soon as you have to compare more than two values, you run into trouble. As the number of wedges increase, the percentages get smaller and smaller, and therefore their size decreases. More colours are needed to uniquely identify each segment. As the chart gets more and more cluttered, it becomes necessary to label not only what the wedges represent but also their values. At this point, you have pretty much recreated some tablular data with a ugly dot in the middle, not to mention that you are now using more space and more pixels than just a list. What extra value is gained from the visual aspects of the pie chart? Relative sizes perhaps, but when they are all thin slivers of tiny percentages differentiated only at the decimal point, does the chart tell a story or is it just eye candy? Can you remove it and have nothing change?

100% or bust!

The values displayed in a pie chart must represent all the answers for a single question. This might sound obvious, but there have been pie charts broadcast on television which add up to more than one hundred per cent. This is impossible! If you have reached this outcome, then you obviously have a problem.

This mistake is probably attributable to the survey consisting of three separate questions that became illustrated in the wrong type of chart. The people polled were asked about their opinion on several topics and responded to each.

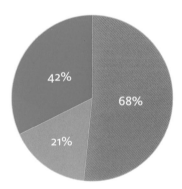

- Q1: Would you support Candidate 1 if he ran for office? (yes/no)
- Q2: Would you support Candidate 2 if she ran for office? (yes/no)
- Q3: Would you support Candidate 3 if he ran for office? (yes/no)

Instead of making three pie charts, one for each question, the 'yes' counts for all three questions were put into a single pie chart. Since the questions were discrete, the values of the answers don't add up to one hundred per cent. In these instances, a pie chart isn't the correct way to display the data: it just doesn't make sense!

Doughnut chart

I'd like to meet the person who thought that a doughnut chart was a good idea. Someone took a pie chart with all its failings and then had the brilliant idea to cut the middle out! Now, it does save on ink, so that is one thing in its favour, but it offers absolutely nothing more than the pie chart.

I wonder if it was once added into a software package as a feature and it stuck. It is hard to remove features once they are in there, and as soon as one package had doughnut charts, everyone had to have doughnut charts. Sometimes it's better to have fewer choices and focus on the charts that best convey the story. A doughnut chart is not one of these.

By removing the centre of a pie chart, it further hinders the ability to judge the weight of each segment. Moving from a healthy wedge to two arcs makes it harder for people to comprehend what value is represented. We know that a full pie chart is one hundred per cent and that any wedge is a fraction of that; if we are presented with only an arc, is it equivalent to the wedge, or is it less because it is missing a portion?

Here the full wedge represents 45% compared to just the arc which also represents 45%. But the volume is very different between them. Are they really equal?

If you create doughnut charts after reading this, I'll hunt you down!

Stacked pie charts

The doughnut chart might well have emerged after the invention of the stacked pie chart. The intention here was to create concentric rings of overlapping wedges to show some sort of data comparison. For example, an inner pie chart could represent the percentage of regional growth in the first quarter and an outer pie chart shows percentage growth in the second quarter. Let's have a look at why this is poor design for pie charts.

First, parts of the lower pie chart are necessarily obscured by placing the second chart on top. And if the inner pie chart is removed to leave the area empty we are back to the doughnut.

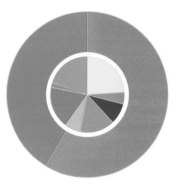

You can quickly see how difficult it is to compare the two rings. Only the first and last wedges are anchored to the same angle; the light-green inner wedge can easily be compared to the outer blue because they both start at the same place. In the outer ring, the blue wedge is much bigger, though a reader still needs to estimate how much bigger. But how much larger is the outer blue wedge compared to the purple one on the other side of the inner pie chart? It is very hard to tell because they don't share a common starting point or even a common side. First, the purple wedge must be rotated until it reaches the same starting place, and then we can estimate its difference to the previous wedge. This is very complicated and could easily be avoided using a different type of chart.

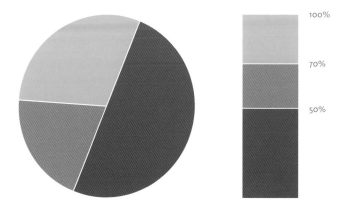

The same relative values in a pie chart can easily be converted to a stacked bar chart without losing any data and increasing readability.

Secondly, stacking pie charts leaves you with more design questions than answers. When one set of represented data overlaps another, how much should be left exposed? How thick should the outer ring be?

A pie chart is designed so that the area of the wedge represents a percentage. When a hole is punched in the middle, the relative percentages of what is left remain the same; since each wedge's area was reduced by the same relative amount, nothing changes. However, if we now compare the inner pie chart's wedges with those of the outer pie chart, the arc might be similar, but the area is not.

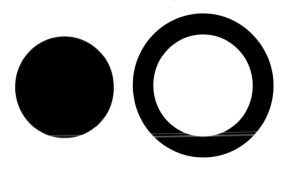

The circle on the left in the figure above has a radius of 50 pixels. Using the formula πr^2 we can work out the area of the circle: in this case $50 \times 50 \times 3.14 = 7{,}850$ pixels. The ring on the right has a radius of 70.71 pixels. Square that and multiply by pi: 15,700 – twice as much as with a radius of 50 pixels. The white cut-out is the area of the black circle; the shaded black areas are equal, but you'd never realize just by looking. It doesn't mean you're bad at geometry, it's just that human brains aren't optimized for figuring out area. When layering pie charts not only are the arcs hard to compare, but also the pixels.

3-D and perspective

With the advent of computer-aided design, fewer and fewer people sit down at a draftsman's table and create with a pencil an isometric mechanical drawing or blueprint. Now, I'm not advocating a return to this analog technology, but some aspects of three-dimensional drawing that once had to be taught are now had for free with a computer.

A perfect example is the perspective vanishing point. This is the point on the horizon that all the 3-D lines lead back to.

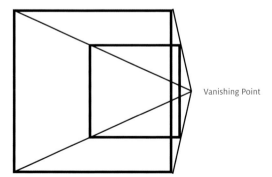

Vanishing Point

When building 3-D pie charts, there is also a vanishing point. This skews the shape of the pie.

So even though the wedges closest to and furthest away from us are the same value, they are very different shapes and sizes. This is not ideal when trying to explain the values with as little bias as possible.

Projecting a pie chart in this way gives an arbitrary height to the closer wedges, thereby adding more pixels to their weight without actually adding more value into their count.

Now, you might be thinking, who would ever go this far to trick the reader? Well, there's a great article called "Lies, Damn Lies and Steve Jobs keynotes" by Jack Schofield in *The Guardian* newspaper[1]. In the article, Schofield highlights the Apple keynote in which Steve Jobs explained how well the sales of the iPhone were coming along. He used the Keynote® presentation software, which allows for crazy 3-D pie charts.

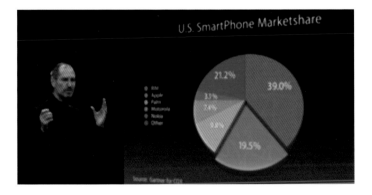

---

[1] http://www.guardian.co.uk/technology/blog/2008/jan/21/liesdamnliesandstevejobs

As you can see, there are six wedges; sales of the iPhone are illustrated by the green wedge that has been pulled away from the rest. Since the pie chart is displayed in three dimensions on a flat screen, the data appears distorted. The front part of the pie chart looks closer and therefore larger than the back. Conveniently, Apple's 19.5% share is at the front, making it look significantly bigger than the 21.2% in the back, which is larger in value, but smaller in pixels.

There is no doubt that the design of this pie chart was conceived to intentionally mislead the viewer. Three-dimensional projects make this very easy to accomplish and, once you realize this, you will begin to see it everywhere.

A simple, more truthful solution would be to convert this pie chart into a simple bar chart.

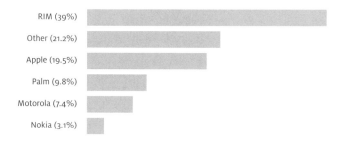

This solves the issues of colour, scale, size, proximity and labels. It isn't as flashy and colourful, but it more accurately reflects the reality of the situation.

Highlighting specific data

As discussed in chapter 7, there are several different ways to highlight a subset of the data to draw more attention to it. There are a few techniques that can be used when dealing with pie charts, such as colour, location and shape.

To highlight just one region, it is possible to mute or remove all the colours except on the single wedge under consideration. It is also possible to explode the pie chart and pull one of the pieces away from the circle. By moving the location, even slightly, the brain makes a distinction.

Even though I've tried to convince you why 3-D pie charts are inappropriate, perhaps you're determined (or obliged) to use them. If so, then it is possible to extend the shape of the wedge vertically so that it is taller than the other pieces. This isn't recommended because of all the distortion issues of 3-D objects in two dimensions. Furthermore, in chapter 11 we talked about how to deceive with data and that 3-D objects take up a greater volume and therefore assume a greater value than what ought to be represented.

At this point, I hope I have demonstrated how pie charts are often more of a hindrance than a help. Their shape, the amount of data they can encode, the number of variables: all are very restrictive. Even though the pie chart is a very common chart, you shouldn't pick it out of your designer tool box too often. As we'll see next, however, there are a few situations in which a round chart style does excel.

Pie charts and time

There are a few instances where a circular chart is useful. The best example is when we are discussing time and clocks. It is possible to use our knowledge of a clock face and adapt a pie chart so instead of expressing one hundred per cent of something, it can represent portions of twelve or twenty-four hours.

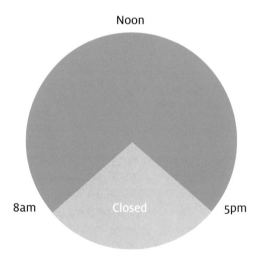

As a circular diagram, it is easy to understand that the store is open from 8am to 5pm, but a problem arises when the opening hours need to be extended. What would a circular diagram look like if you were open from 8am to 10pm? Now you have an overlap! If you are going to use this technique instead of a simple table of opening and closing times, you'd better do it right!

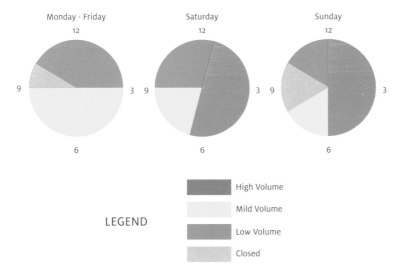

IKEA used these circular clock face diagrams to explain its opening hours and the customer traffic levels; this allowed shoppers to decide when to visit the store based on how many other customers were there. (There are several problems dealing with the psychology of publishing this information and how it affects the decisions of the shoppers, but that's another book entirely.)

If we look at the IKEA examples, they're a good first start. The diagrams make use of our knowledge of the clock face to represent opening times. So far so good, but the labelling could be confusing. Is '6', 6am or 6pm? On Saturday, what time does the store open? You could assume 9am, but then the graph isn't actually telling you a story: you are just jumping to a conclusion.

There is an easy solution to fix some of these ambiguities: convert the round clock-like chart into a horizontal stacked bar chart. Time is read from left to right, so nothing is lost in the conversion. We now know when the shop opens – that's the leftmost point – and we've relabelled "12" as "noon". Using the 24-hour clock is another alternative.

Monday - Friday

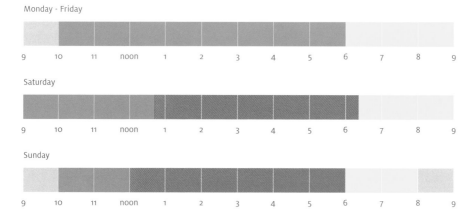

Saturday

Sunday

9   10   11   noon   1   2   3   4   5   6   7   8   9

Roll out those circles

Any pie chart can be converted into a much more useful and
readable stacked bar chart. When a pie chart seems to be a bad
idea, it can be 'rolled out' into something better. Imagine rolling
the wheel of the pie chart and leaving a trace on the ground. The
length of that line is equivalent to the circumference of the wheel.
Don't worry, no maths needed here.

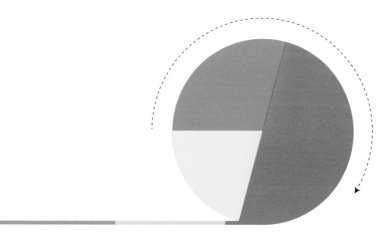

Now we can see the portions of the pie chart as relative rectangular lengths. This rolled out pie chart still shows all the data, and the pieces within it are much easier to compare and reorder without having to do any mental rotation of the wedges.

Who ate my pie?

One situation in which a pie chart completely falls down is with negative numbers. Let's say a large corporation wants to create a pie chart of its annual income, broken down by each division. If there are five divisions, what would a pie chart look like if their incomes were as follows?

A = 2,000
B = 3,000
C = 500
D = -300
E = 2,300

This is very easy to represent as a bar chart, because values below zero can be drawn; as a pie chart, it is almost impossible. All of the profits can be represented, but how is division D's loss accounted for? A pie wedge can't overlap another to demonstrate negative income.

Microsoft's Excel simply plots the negative value as positive in a pie chart, but labels it as negative. Dealing with this issue is so problematic, however, that it is best to just avoid it altogether by selecting a more appropriate chart type.

Decagraph

If you must use a pie chart, then you should consider a decagraph. It follows the exact same rules as a pie chart, but instead of having a circular border, its shape is that of a decagon – a ten-sided figure. This has the advantage of each corner representing ten per cent.

Every wedge is somewhere between these ten per cent markers, making it easier to gauge the correct value.

I don't know many charting applications that have decagraphs among their default options, but it is something to consider when designing and developing your own charts. Adding corners to a circle adds more information and can remove pixels.

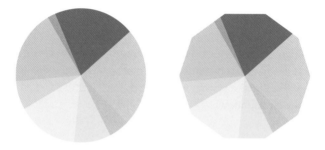

Sexagesimal ~ http://en.wikipedia.org/wiki/Sexagesimal

We're all familiar with base-10 counting systems; our ten fingers and ten toes, plus the Arabic numeral system, make it an obvious and powerful method of calculation. You're probably also aware of base-16 when you deal with hex colours on the web: FF = 255, A0 = 160 and so on. In chapter 10 we looked at how to convert base-10 into base-16 when using Dopplr's colouring algorithm. A computer's logic uses base-2 with ones and zeros. From binary we can build up very complex systems.

Sexagesimal is base-60. This might seem strange and in no way useful, but humans have used it in various forms for thousands of years, most notably on the clock face.

Sexagesimal systems can be divided by whole numbers in twelve different ways. The factors are: 1, 2, 3, 4, 5, 6, 10, 12, 15, 20, 30 and 60. This means that you can take any of those values and divide them into 60 and get a whole number back. There are sixty minutes in an hour, and it can be divided into twelve sections of five, to mark the twelve hours in each half of the day. We often refer to quarter-hours, since each hour can be divided into four fifteen-minute portions.

Old coins and armband jewellery were also ridged and broken into these units. A coin that has twelve bits can be split between two, three, four and six people evenly. Base-60 sounds complicated, but it makes for a very flexible system when dividing goods, services and time between groups of various sizes.

Encoding a second variable

A pie chart depicts a list of items and their relative percentage values; that's only one variable per item. When we look for ways to add a second variable for each wedge, we quickly hit a wall.

Since each wedge in a pie chart is unique and touching its immediate neighbours, distinct colours are needed for each one. If not, we run the risk of juxtaposed wedges sharing the same colour and it being impossible to tell where one starts and the other stops. We've also previously investigated other ways to encode additional variables with limited success.

Company Departments by Gender

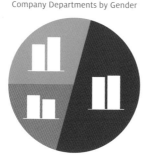

It is possible to put a chart on a chart, but that is just a disaster waiting to happen. The only good solutions to encoding a second variable in pie charts are extending the wedges in two dimensions, or something called a belt chart. We'll discuss extending the wedges in chapter 22 when we discuss polar area charts.

Belt chart

A belt chart is a series of concentric rings, each ring representing a percentage of the area of the previous, inner ring – it is almost as confusing as it sounds. For example in the charts below, the innermost white circle represents all of the participants in the Olympics. In the left chart, the next ring out represents the proportion of participants from each of the five populated continents (North America, South America, Australia, Africa and Eurasia – hence the five rings in the Olympic symbol). We can then move to the outer ring to see the gender breakdown by continent. Adding up all the women participants by continent would give the total of women participants in the Olympics. Each ring represents a different statistic, but remains related to the overall percentage. This isn't a true second variable, like funding per nation; for that we'd need to look into 2-D wedge scaling.

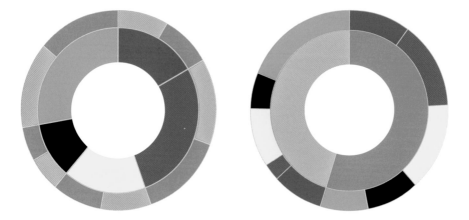

As you can see, this example ends up looking like a psychedelic poker chip! We can go on and on too. Imagine a third ring, where each of the blue or pink wedges would be broken down by age, which itself could have a fourth ring, and so on.

The order is not important, although it's easier to focus on one aspect above another. As we can see on the right, our first ring could have been gender, so there is only one pink and one blue wedge. The second ring shows the breakdown by continent, displaying two red, blue, green, yellow and black wedges, one each for males and females. It all depends on the story you want to tell.

Much like the treemap, each inner segment or arc represents the total of its outer children, so it is possible to drill down into each section to get another view. In the treemap this characteristic would need to be animated or displayed on a separate chart, as otherwise the data gets cluttered with tiny boxes, each with a border to keep its data contained. With the radial tree chart this is achieved by adding another ring. Each ring is a breakdown of what is inside the parent.

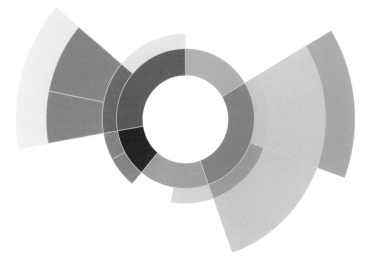

Just looking at this diagram makes my eyes hurt. I can see how many rings deep the structure is and see plenty of tiny slivers at the edges, but I can't make any logical comparisions. Looking at the inner segments, the red one makes up perhaps thirty per cent of the total. As we move outward, most of what makes up that thirty per cent is four levels deep. The size of that block is much larger at the fourth level than the first, yet it represents less information. This means that you can't compare a wedge in one level to a wedge in another. You need to first figure out what percentage that wedge shows in its ring, then look at the other wedge, figure out what percentage that shows in its ring, and only then compare the two. At this point, you're better off looking it up in a table.

Dealing with a circular visualization and trying to compare its radial portions is always problematic. When designing with data, the story should always be told as clearly as possible. To do so, it is often best to avoid round charts and graphs.

20

SCATTER PLOTS

Scatter plots are a useful tool to reveal relationships between any
amount of independent values. A scatter plot is like a line graph,
but without the connecting lines. The data points are placed in a
grid in an attempt to build a larger picture.

Two values that correlate well in life are age and height.
You start your early years small and grow until you reach your
adult height.

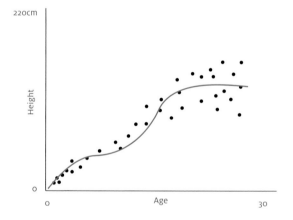

This creates a nice trend line because age and height have a
relationship, but not everything does. For instance, we can take
the square kilometers of a country's area and its population.

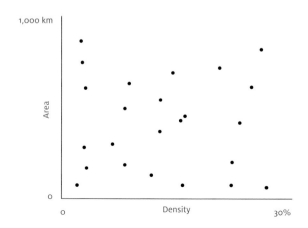

Some countries have a very dense population per square kilometer and some do not. There are some countries with a large population and large area, some countries with a large area and low population, and some with high population and low area and everything in between. There is no general trend line.

This is just fictitious data; with proper information, a trend might be found, or an ideal zone that few countries break out of. If conditions get too bad in any one country, people might emigrate and so reveal a critical point. Also, this chart won't be complete until the data points are labelled; the chart isn't that interesting until we know who's who.

These sorts of scatter plots have their origin at zero, since all the values are positive numbers. But it's possible to create graphs that extend past the zero point in both directions. Some people might call this a Cartesian coordinate system; some people might just call this a table: for simplicity, let's call it a matrix.

Matrix

This matrix is a two-dimensional grid that extends in both positive and negative directions from the origin. It provides a two-dimensional space to plot data.

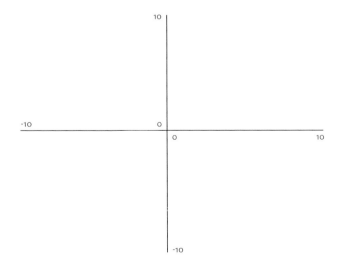

It could extend into a third dimension to represent a third
variable, but such a diagram could become confusing and difficult
to understand.

When building a matrix, it's important to put opposed
attributes at each end of the axes. This is straightforward when
dealing with numbers – you can go right to positive 10 and left to
negative 10 – but non-numerical information can be displayed
too. Let's take a look at a matrix presenting potential vacation
options.

On your vacation you could visit locations nearby or you
could travel further away. Against that we could plot the strengths
of local currencies, but that is just a numeric scale like –10 to
+10. Instead we'll plot distance against the complexities of travel
paperwork and visas.

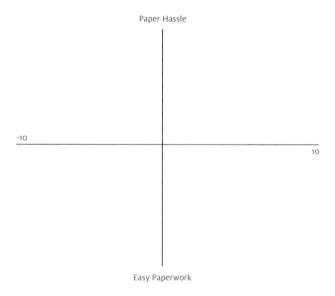

The left side of the matrix, labelled 'near', represents potential
holiday spots close to home. On the opposite side of this is 'far'.
Only you can judge what these terms mean and which locations
are too near or far to be close to the sweet spot at the centre.

Maybe it isn't distance that's at stake here, but rather the time it takes to get somewhere. This gives you a range of places to visit based on perceived distance and travel time.

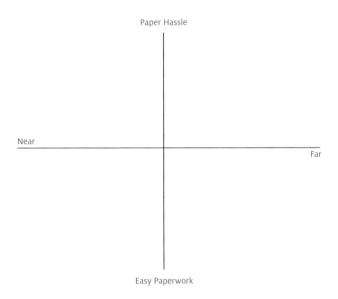

Based on simple distance, New York could be considered near Quebec, London near Moscow, Tokyo close to Beijing, Jerusalem near Cairo – but each of these cities might cause different paperwork headaches for the traveller. At the far end of the spectrum, assuming a start point of London, UK, far away places might included Sydney, Australia or Rio de Janeiro, Brazil. While both of these cities are distant, there could be direct flights from London making them straightforward to visit, so they aren't placed as far away on the matrix.

Now we need to add in the second variable, the bureaucratic hassle while you're preparing for your trip. This is based on your nationality, your passport status, health precautions and how strict each country is about tourists. At the top of the matrix we'll place countries with stringent criteria and at the bottom those which are more relaxed. Starting from London, if your destination is a city within the UK, then the data point can be put at the very bottom, since you don't have to check your passport or deal with visas – though public transport might be a factor in the distance stakes!

Within the European Union member states, citizens can travel relatively easily, so a trip from London to Paris is both close and very relaxed. The data point for Paris can go in the lower-left quadrant. Alternatively, travelling from London to New York City involves a regular seven-hour flight, so it might be placed just within the near category, but for non-US citizens there can be a mountain of paperwork to fill out before arriving. Therefore, New York could be put in the upper-left quadrant: it is relatively close, but has strict rules for tourists.

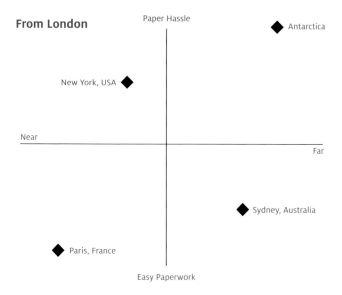

A further-flung destination such as Sydney, Australia is straightforward for a British citizen to visit. Therefore, Sydney finds itself in the lower-right quadrant: it is far away, but has relaxed rules for British tourists. The last quadrant might be filled with more exotic places like Antarctica – as a scientific base, visiting as a tourist would require a few questions to be answered! Travelling to some South American or Asian countries will require a raft of vaccinations. Such places would be put into the upper-right quadrant: far away and a hassle.

Now, rather than just a list of potential destinations and their paperwork requirements, we have plotted them on to a matrix, making it much easier to see the outliers and any clusters. We can also see if there are any areas which are empty or completely ignored.

Anyone working on a business plan has probably done something similar with a SWOT analysis (Strengths versus Weaknesses, Opportunities versus Threats). By placing strengths and weaknesses on one scale, threats and opportunities on the other, almost any scenario can be plotted into the matrix and ideally help build a better company.

It's also useful to use matrices to plot a company against its competitors. If a company finds itself in the low end market and unpopular, it might want to adjust its brand image to make its products more popular. By plotting all of the competition into a matrix, it's possible to work out who needs to be imitated or how a company can differentiate itself.

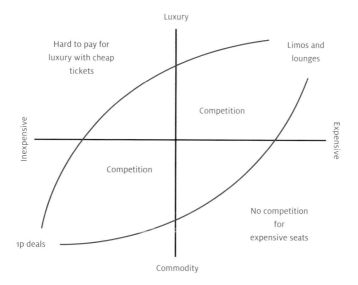

It can also be a good indicator of gaps in the market. Maybe no one is catering to the low-end market and someone could move in and grab a portion of the revenue. The airline industry could plot expensive versus inexpensive and luxury versus commodity. Some airlines pick up their customers in a limousine, offer lounge access and treat passengers like royalty; these airlines would sit in the high luxury/high price quadrant of the matrix. Then there are plenty of companies in the low quality/low price quadrant. (We've all probably been suckered into their one penny deals! The old adage rings true: you get what you pay for.) There are probably very few companies that are expensive and low quality. The sweet spot is an ideal amount of luxury compared to price. Most airlines would probably fall inside the two curves.

Nolan chart

The Nolan chart is a very specific type of scatter plot matrix. It is used to determine political standing and plots economic freedom against personal freedoms. Really, though, a Nolan chart is just a scatter plot under a different name with a single purpose.

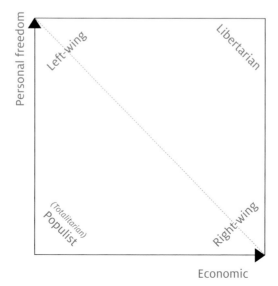

Bubble chart

So far we've looked at a scatter plot as a matrix comparing two variables. These get encoded in into the axes as positive and negative numbers or attributes. But what if we wanted to explore encoding more variables – maybe price, luxury and a third: availability.

The bubble chart is a specific type of scatter plot that makes use of size to encode a third variable. Each data point is mapped onto the axes and then the size of each point is scaled up or down depending on the third variable.

With a small set of data, it becomes immediately apparent which of the values is the largest, but when the set increases in size, the chart could become cluttered with overlapping data points, with larger dots covering or obscuring smaller ones, affecting the interpretation of the values.

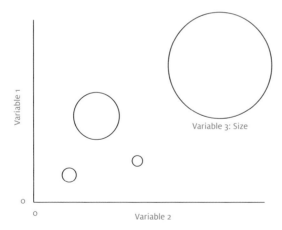

This type of chart might be called a bubble chart, but the third variable need not be a bubble. In chapter 7 we discussed several ways to draw attention to particular items of data and we can use these ideas again here. We could try different shapes for each data point, different colours, or different sizes. It's also possible to make combinations of colour and shape to encode fourth and fifth variables. But be warned: you'll soon be treading on the thin ice of chart junk.

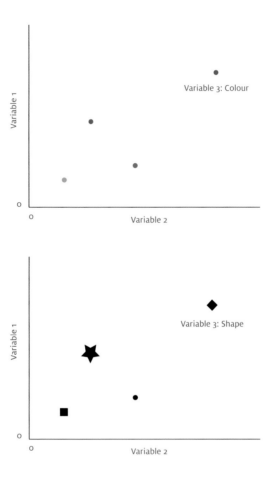

Some practitioners have taken the bubble chart and made it dynamic by including time – they call this a motion chart – to form an animated series of bubble charts. The most famous examples come from Hans Rosling, a Swedish Professor of International Health and Director of the Gapminder Foundation. Using bubble charts, he has mapped out multiple variables such as child mortality, GDP and population. When put together into a motion chart, the fourth variable, time, makes for a very interesting show'. The bubbles grow and shrink, and move around the matrix; as countries get wealthier, their child mortality drops and their populations increase. Static bubble charts and scatter plots can only provide one frame of this animation at a time, whereas the motion chart tells a much more interesting story.

Summary

You now know much more about the basic types of charts found in most applications. The perennial line graph, bar chart, area chart, pie chart and scatter plot have all been examined and explained in great detail. They were once just tiny icons in a sea of options, but I hope that you now know a lot more about which is appropriate for your data and when.

In the final section, we're going to look at some less common charts and graphs. These are lumped together for several reasons. In some cases they are uncommon because they have quite specific purposes, in others because they are difficult to use correctly, or just difficult to immediately comprehend as a chart. The purpose of walking through these more unusual charts is to spark some new ideas and encourage you to break away from the common types of charts.

Now that you know how to use the regular graphs and charts, it's time to push the boundaries a bit and see what else is possible.

---

[1] http://www.ted.com/talks/hans_rosling_shows_the_best_stats_you_ve_ever_seen.html

Part 5

Not so common charts

So far, we've talked about the history of charts and graphs, issues of colour and ink, the ability to mislead with data and some common types of charts and graphs. Now I want to talk about some of the less common types. They are less common not because they are poorly designed; as we saw, pie charts are popular even though their design often fails to convey the information properly. Rather, these less usual charts have gone mostly unnoticed or are used for very specific purposes. By introducing them here, I hope to make you aware of certain problems to avoid in your own designs and show you other interesting opportunities to illustrate your data.

Maps, choropleths and cartograms

Radar plots

Gauges and thermometers

Sound

Everything and the kitchen sink

MAPS, CHOROPLETHS AND CARTOGRAMS

You probably don't think of maps as charts or graphs, but
they do serve as a very specific type. Much like grids and axes
define boundaries on a line graph, a map defines geographical
boundaries into which the rest of the data flows.

We can take a table of place names, latitudes and longitudes
and plot them on a map. Think of this in the same way you would
with an X and Y plot.

Name	Latitude	Longitude
Edinburgh	55°56'58"N	3°9'37"W
Newcastle	54°58'N	1°36'W
Manchester	53°28'N	2°14'W
Cardiff	51°29'07"N	3°11'12"W
London	51°30'29"N	0°7'29"W

For geographical data sets, a map is an obvious choice. If you are
exploring weather data, earthquake information, postal code
mapping, or other geographically specific information, plotting it
to latitude and longitude makes sense, but you need to be aware of
a few drawbacks.

Scaling

The scale of a map can cause problems when large and small areas are compared simultaneously. On a map of the US, the smaller New England states tend to be exploded and scaled up just to make sure their data is visible when compared to the map of the rest of the country. The political boundaries on a map can also become problematic when scaled. A border that is one pixel in width is fine when the output is very large, but as it gets smaller, that one pixel border takes up a larger proportion of the overall design, leading to clutter and confusion. We discussed the data to pixel ratio in chapter 6, as well as some ways to lighten up the grid lines, all of which also applies to map borders.

Sometimes scaling cannot be avoided, but there are options other than exploding a part of the map to an inset box at a different scale. Different map projections can be explored.

Map projections

A map projection is a method of transposing a three-dimensional surface, such as that of the Earth, into two dimensions. Maps of the Earth come in many well-known projections, from Mercator to Buckminster Fuller's famous Dymaxion, Albers to sinusoidal. Each attempt to solve the problem of mapping three dimensions to two has advantages and drawbacks, but sometimes maps are distorted for other reasons.

Dymaxion projection

Worldmapper[1] creates maps where each country is resized and reshaped in accordance with a particular variable. The more distorted the shape of the country is, the higher or lower the value. The example below shows population density. The more people within the country's borders, the greater the distortion.

When the regions of a map are distorted in order to convey more meaning, this is referred to as a cartogram. It is a specific type of map data design.

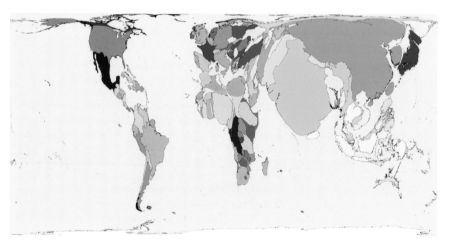

© Copyright 2009 SASI Group (University of Sheffield)

Like the issues around comparing the sizes of pie chart wedges (see chapter 19), relative national landmass areas cannot be judged accurately without a comparison to the original map. If the change is only slight, then it might be unnoticeable, but if the scale wasn't known in the first place, how can the change be understood? If a large country such as Brazil was increased in size by 1.2% would the difference be noticeable? If so, could anyone tell that it was 1.2% rather than 1%? Probably not. Even when the change is large and obvious, a 400% increase will still be difficult to distinguish

[1]   http://www.sasi.group.shef.ac.uk/worldmapper/

from a 378% increase. These sorts of distortions work well as a
visual effect, but not for conveying actual statistical data.

When we zoom into smaller regions within maps, they too are
distorted on purpose. Have you ever really looked closely at a map
of your city? Some features are emphasized and others reduced in
importance, but this is acceptable because such maps are designed
for specific purposes more than for geographic accuracy. A map is
not a satellite photograph.

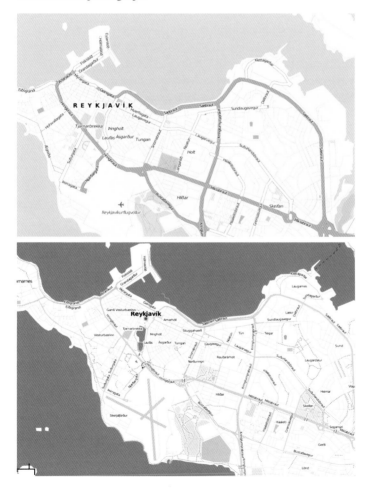

Take street widths, for instance. Street maps display different kinds of streets at different line widths. These are not to scale by any means, but we tend not to worry that main thoroughfares are wider on the map and side streets are smaller, while retaining their correct positions on the map. Streets are not scaled based on their physical size, but instead based on the type of thoroughfare. This distortion helps the reader understand which streets are the major and minor roads by their representation on the map.

There are other reasons that some maps 'lie' about the real world to aid comprehension in the viewer. A perfect example of this is the famous London Underground map. It is not laid out with geographical accuracy, but instead is based on the relative position of the stations. While we might think this is a somewhat new and unusual idea – Harry Beck's map was drawn in 1931 and first published in 1933, less than a century ago – it goes back a lot further.

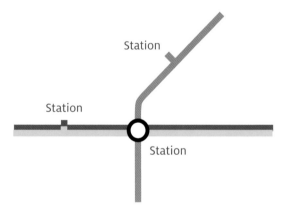

In 1804, the American West was newly purchased from France and the US government needed to know precisely what it had bought. President Jefferson selected US Army Captain Meriwether Lewis to lead the expedition to explore the new territory. Fellow soldier William Clark joined the expedition at Lewis's request. The Lewis and Clark expedition was the first overland expedition to explore the new territory in search of the Pacific Ocean, mapping as it went. Sacagawea and other Native American Indians helped Lewis and Clark travel across this new land by guiding them and supplying local maps of their areas.

Lewis and Clark found the maps the Native Americans provided very confusing. They were quite unlike the European maps the surveyors were used to, consisting of landmarks placed relative only to each other. Travelling down a river, the Native Americans were worried less about the turns and bends it might make than about the landmarks they passed. These markers formed the basis of navigation. Similarly, when travelling on the London Underground, the New York City subway or other mass-transit systems, a passenger needs to know how many stations lie between their starting station and their intended destination, and where to change lines rather than the precise geographical location of either.

Once you have chosen your map projection, you need to lay out the grid in which your data will flow. Maybe the data is just the landmarks on the map. In that case, you're finished, but maybe you have additional data about each region which needs to be displayed.

Applying a single data variable to a map

Single variable data corresponds to one value. For instance, if you want to show which of the US states voted Republican (red) or Democratic (blue), it is a simple binary decision. A given region can be turned on or off by filling in the boundary with a single colour. While the colours blue and red were chosen because they represent the two parties, the same information could be displayed with ink and no ink.

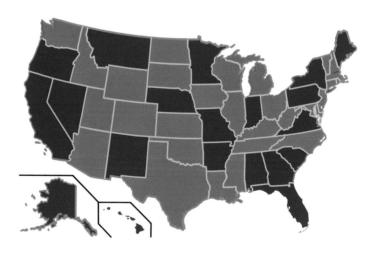

Applying a single variable to a map is the simplest way to start, but the world is rarely black and white: rather, it is many shades of grey. The next step, then, is to create a gradient of colour for the data to represent a sliding scale of values, and develop a range of colours between red and blue at varying intensities. The purpler the state, the more it was a mixture. It is usually best, however, to use shades of grey from pure black to pure white stepped in between for all the reasons discussed in chapter 9. People with colour-blindness will see this map in similar shades of the same colour. When this illustration is printed in black and white, all the beautiful shades of colour become a diluted grey. It becomes impossible to tell the difference between a light red and a light blue when both values are represented in greyscale. The data becomes unreadable and therefore useless to the reader.

The major downside to using a gradient is that it is difficult to distinguish 83% grey from 80% grey. Sometimes it's useful to group the data into discrete blocks (for example, 100–80%, 79–60%, 59–40%, 39–20%, 19–0%). This has the advantage of clarifying the colour distinctions, but some fine-grained nuances can be lost. By increasing the number of discrete blocks the granularity can be increased, but so can the potential for confusion. Depending on the data, somewhere will be a sweet spot balancing the two, with a few unique colours while still creating enough buckets to describe the data.

Maps that have specific colour-coded regions are referred to as choropleths. Choropleths can be used in conjuction with cartograms and other map styles and projections.

In chapter 9, we discussed the use of colour and a few tips and tricks about what is good and bad. It applies as much to maps as to charts and graphs.

There are other ways besides colour to represent a range of data. Take weather, for instance; it could be sunny, cloudy, raining, snowing, thundery, and so on. This could work in a very similar way to a gradient of colours, as there is a range of possible values which each area falls into. Instead of discrete blocks of colour, however, different icons representing each type of weather are placed on the map as a graphical way to represent information. The weather icons could be replaced with colours – green for rain, red for sun, blue for snow, yellow for clouds – but the choice of colours would be arbitrary and not necessarily make sense. Similarly, the Republican and Democratic areas could be represented with some sort of icon.

If it's not desirable or possible to use a map, you can display geographic data in a list or table. When creating lists, they need to be ordered somehow: alphabetically; numerically by temperature; or by other factors under consideration. A map removes the need to order the values because latitude and longitude underpin their placement.

Name	Weather	Temp
Edinburgh	Cloudy	10°C
Newcastle	Overcast	11°C
Manchester	Overcast	10°C
Cardiff	Sunny	12°C
London	Sunny	12°C

This table of weather information, however, doesn't give you the same effect as a weather forecaster standing in front of a large map.

When enough data points are plotted geographically, trends can begin to emerge. This is as true for weather as for crime statistics and other geographically determined data. It's something that a plain list cannot effectively convey.

Representing multi-variable data on a map

Plotting multi-variable data in a regular grid system with x- and y-axes is easier than plotting on to a geographical map. When adding multi-variable data to a map, different graph types begin to merge together and trouble starts brewing.

One example of merging multi-variable data with latitude and longitude is the addition of a bar chart or pie chart at the corresponding geographical point. It attempts to convey that in a particular area certain statistics have been found. If the bar or pie chart shows only a single variable range, such as Red versus Blue, then the gradient method can be used, but if it contains more than two variables, the chart mixing begins.

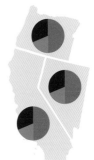

The best way to solve this is to avoid it altogether, or re-evaluate what is required. What is the goal? What story needs to be told? With an answer to those questions, it should be possible to go back and try a different design.

Maps and time

Showing data over time using a map is difficult. We see this most often on weather satellite charts, which animate the weather moving over the map.

It is possible to display single variable data on a map over time using the same gradient technique where white is one value and black a second value. Instead of quantity or intensity being expressed in the gradient between white and black, a rate of change can be conveyed. So, something like the value of property

over a ten year period in a given city can be plotted on a map. As
house prices rose or fell they would be shaded with more white or
black accordingly. Such a chart doesn't describe what the value of
the property was at the start, only that it rose or fell. It is the same
technique used in the treemap in chapter 18.

In a dynamic context, animations can take initial conditions
into account because anyone can scroll back to the earliest
point to see the baseline data and compare it to the data from a
later time.

Maps and geography can also be used in a timeline. A famous
example was created in 1869 by Charles Joseph Minard, describing
Napoleon's 1812 campaign in Russia.

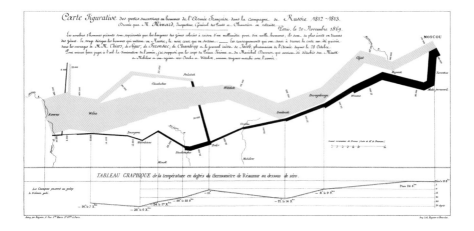

This works very well partly because Napoleon's army marched in a consistent direction, west to east, before retreating east to west. Had Napoleon taken a more complex route, this flow map might not have been possible.

When moving from point to point across the map, time passes. If the line crosses over itself or goes backwards, a gradient can be added so that as time progresses to the end, the line gets darker and darker to demonstrate change.

A map showing volume and direction is called a flow map. Flow maps aren't much used: they are close to the realm of visualizations and infographics. It is hard to determine how many items where shipped from the start and how many ended up at each destination.

22

RADAR PLOTS

Radar plots sometimes go by different names – spider plots, star plots – so don't get confused: they're all the same thing. In a radar plot, lines radiate out from a central point, increasing in value as they move away from the centre; each line represents a single category or aspect of the data. Data points on each arm are connected to the next via a line graph which creates a polygon.

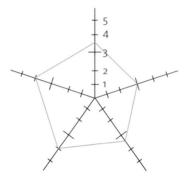

As each of the categories is connected to the others, similar values make for a more even shape. The further from the centre the shape appears, the greater or higher the results. The shape will often vary: it can be small or large, a sort of diamond or something that looks like a wheel of cheese with a chunk taken out of it. You can have fun inventing your own names.

Radar plots work best when they have a small set of attributes. The more arms there are, the more acute the angle between them. With 360 attributes, there will be only one degree for each which, if the data jumps from high to low, could result in a disorienting starburst effect.

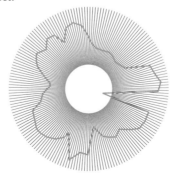

The size and resolution of the radar plot will influence the density of attributes which can be modelled. There is no guideline of how many is too many, so it's best to err on the side of fewer arms. As we'll see later, if you encounter problems with too many attributes, then maybe a radar plot isn't the best graph to use. Maybe a bar chart would be more appropriate.

One argument for the existence of this type of graph is that it works well when overlaid with other radar plots to create a composite image. This provides you with an overview of all the different items being modelled and trends can be easily identified.

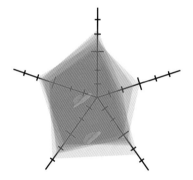

Just like a line graph, a radar plot can contain multiple data sets at once, and all the same problems apply: how to pick distinct colours or (if in black and white) how to pick distinct shapes, and so on. This example uses opacity to let the data sets show through, but this technique works effectively only with a small number of data sets.

All the techniques described in chapter 6 that can reduce the number of pixels also apply to radar plots. Unnecessary axes can be removed, as well as tick marks, the shape can be reduced to only the observed range, and so on. But as we strip away more of what isn't data, problems can emerge.

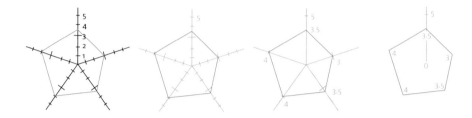

With a line graph or bar chart, the vertical axis only appears
once; with a radar plot, each radial point requires some sort of
demarcation. But what might be more important is just the shape
of the object in comparison to others. If you are keen to convey the
actual values, then shape recognition is of little use but, if you're
just looking to spot the odd ball in a set of data, this could be a
good technique.

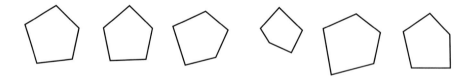

As you can see, test subject four doesn't look like the rest.
It might be possible to miss this in a table of numbers, but the
visualization makes it clear.

Multiscalar plots

Each line radiating from the centre can support its own scale.
While this can be dangerous because few people will immediately
notice the different values, it allows different kinds of data to
be displayed on one chart. For instance, one attribute might be
average rainfall in millimetres, whereas the next attribute might
be average humidity. Two different scales would be required on
the same graph.

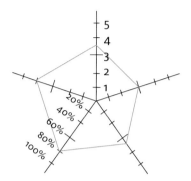

Issues

There are two major problems with the radar plot. First is the difficulty of comparing data across the diameter of the ring. Comparing a value on the second axis with the fourth axis is hindered not only by the distance between them but also because they are rotated in space. A vertical scale at each point is needed to help determine the value. This adds ink and pixels, decreasing the data to pixels ratio. Other chart types rarely have to repeat values on their axes, making this a drawback for radial charts.

The second problem is the distorting effect radar plots have on area. The outermost circumference of a radar plot encompasses a larger area than the innermost circumference, and it therefore acquires added visual weight. The red line connects the value five on all the axes and the blue line marks one on each of the axes. The area within the red line, however, is much more than five times the area within the blue line, yet that is the ratio according to the scale.

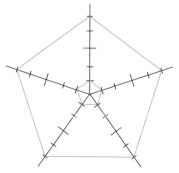

The footprint of a radar plot is usually square even when each of the radial arms is the same length, creating a circle. The height of a radar graph is approximately twice the size of the scale. So if there are ten units, the plot needs to be twenty units in height. This leaves a wasted area around the edges of the chart. Below, this area is shaded to reveal what is not part of the graph, but is still taken up by its footprint. Like the pie chart, there is more wasted space than in other chart types.

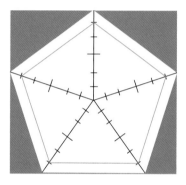

A bar chart of the same data need only be ten units in height because it does not cut an arc around a central point, but instead extends horizontally. Depending on the number of values, the width can be less than the corresponding radar plot. If our goal is to reduce the data to pixel ratio, then as much cruft as possible needs to be eliminated.

Often information on a radar plot can be illustrated more clearly on a bar chart. It's much easier to read and takes up less space when comparing a low number of values on the same scale.

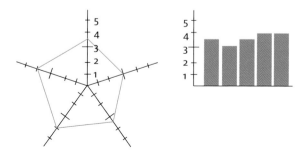

Since order is not in itself significant in a radar plot, the same as a bar chart, we can rearrange the values to make the order best suit the circumstances; maybe it is best to reference the data alphabetically, or by region, or from least to greatest.

Extra care needs to be taken with radar plots containing different scales on each arm, as these may need to become separate bar charts. In the previous weather example, we couldn't put average rainfall in millimetres on the same bar chart as average humidity, but they can be displayed on independent bar charts.

When overlaying radar plots, it can be useful to take averages of all the values and display them on a bar chart. This is much more empirical than making the viewer guess at what the averages might be from sight.

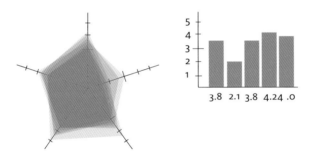

It doesn't create as pretty a picture, but the goal of your design is to tell the data's story, not let the reader make an incorrect interpretation.

Polar area diagram

The polar area diagram was invented by Florence Nightingale in 1858 as an aid to describing her experiences in the Crimean War. It is sometimes used synonymously with the term coxcomb. This is because Nightingale referred to a compilation of these diagrams as a coxcomb and the term later became attached to the diagrams themselves. As a nurse during the war she tried to improve the living conditions of hospitalized soldiers. Many died from infections and other non-battle-related injuries. At the time, ending up in hospital actually increased a soldier's chances of dying due to poor hygienic conditions.

In a report that she produced for the British government, Nightingale outlined all the different causes of death during several months of the war. This was represented in the diagram below:

Diagram of the Causes of Mortality in the Army in the East

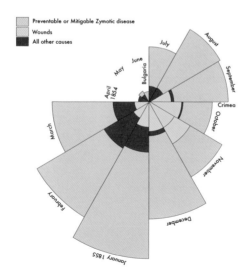

The black line across November 1854 marks the boundry of the deaths from all other causes during that month. In October 1854, the black coincides with the red.

Florence Nightingale 1856

It was a very early visualization, so I won't fault her for her efforts, but there are several improvements that could be made to the design. First, this isn't actually a stacked area graph: the bars are hidden behind each other. This is why she makes the notes about months November, October and April. The chart attempts to compare data both within the same month and to each of the other months.

Is anything gained by telling this story in the round? Or should the data be converted into a bar chart? There are two options: an area chart showing all of the casualties and the breakdown by each type; or three separate bars for each month. Each tells a slightly different story.

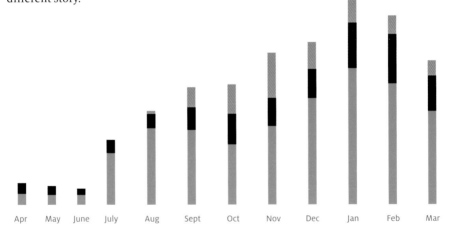

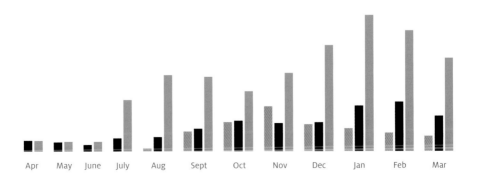

Both options make the values and the relationships between them clearer. The eye can more easily imagine a horizontal line across the tops of the bars rather than an arc around the circle to try and compare different months' values.

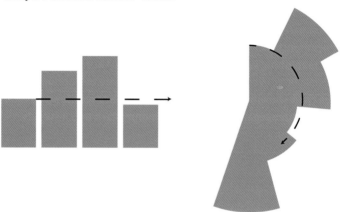

Florence Nightingale introduced a new type of chart, even though her data might have been better conveyed in a bar chart. There are several legitimate uses for polar diagrams, such as the wind rose which we'll look at next. Without her contribution, it might have been many more years before polar area diagrams were discovered.

Wind rose

This is a type of circular chart that is less like a radar chart and more of a representation of the data in a geographical form. The wind rose displays wind speed and direction. The center of the circle represents the point at which the measurements were taken and the points radiating out follow the points of the compass. In this example, the chart measures average wind speed over a set period of time.

Wind speed (m/s) by direction

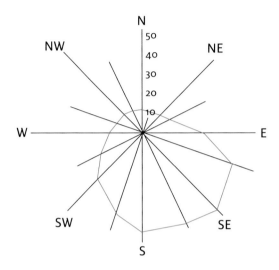

You can easily see the prevailing wind direction is south-southeast. We understand this chart because we are used to a spacial world. When we stand outside looking north, we act as the centre of the wind rose. We intuitively understand the intensity and frequency of the wind from this diagram. It is actually a very specific type of map, showing not political borders, but relative spacial position. The length of the bars could represent different attributes such as wind speed, air temperature or intensity of sunlight falling on the detector.

This is a good chart design to have in your toolbox. It is very specific, and fills a unique niche in spacial representations.

23 GAUGES AND THERMOMETERS

Measuring devices that are not usually professionally employed to show progress levels are the gauge and thermometer. If this is the voice you want to speak with, then maybe thermometers are for you, but generally they equate to kitsch chart junk.

Thermometers

Charity fundraisers like to use thermometers to show the progress of donations. Next time you see a thermometer used in this way, ask yourself, "What is this thermometer actually showing?" They attempt to show two things: progress and quantity. Over time, people can see the progress of the thermometer rising towards the top, which is the target amount. It also shows us the current quantity pledged toward the goal.

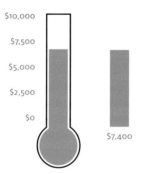

It is really two distinct possible charts. It could be as simple as a bar chart with a single bar – the vertical axis is the quantity pledged. This is exactly the same as the thermometer, but without the chart junk bulb at the bottom and extra design of the thermometer itself.

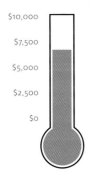
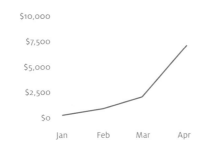

The thermometer is also trying to be a line graph. Over time, contributions are added to the pool, thereby increasing the height of the thermometer reading. This has the same effect as adding data points to the line graph as the time passes. The line graph's vertical axis is the amount pledged. Over time it rises, which also lets us look back at any given date and see the amount. It could be that just before the end of the tax year more donations are received, or perhaps around holidays or major promotional activity. With a single bar or thermometer, this interesting data is lost.

Gauges and dials

There have been whole books written on these topics. Most agree that gauges and dials are a bad idea! For an excellent resource, see *Information Dashboard Design: The Effective Visual Communication of Data* by Stephen Few.

If we ignore the use of nineteenth century-style steam gauges in a digital world, the chart junk and other unnecessary pixels should instantly alert us to a few problems. The new generation of people coming to computers has probably never seen a five and a quarter inch floppy disk, or even a three and half inch disk, yet many of our applications' save icons use this metaphor.

It looks somewhat outdated now: imagine how it will look in five to ten years. But we still persist with dashboard gauges that are not only from a past era, but pointless.

Dials and gauges present a similar problem to pie charts and other radial diagrams: comparing separated values with different orientations is difficult to accomplish. Without the labels, would anyone understand that the needle has moved from zero to seventy? The angle would have to be estimated and converted to the approriate scale, and the value would have to be guessed at. Presenting the value on its own would be much more straightforward and informative.

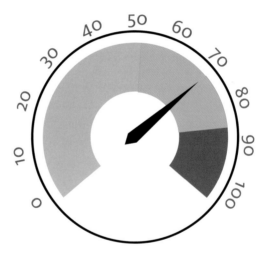

Not only that, but there are many wasted pixels as this is a circular diagram. A round gauge uses only the circular area to convey data, but a square shape is taken up within the flow of the document. This means that over 21% of the pixels are wasted.

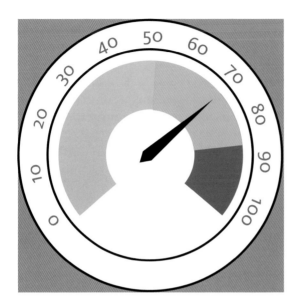

(4 × 4 units square = 16 square units. Circle = pi × 22 = 12.4. Subtracting the circle's area from the square's leaves 3.4 which is 21.4% of the area)

The same information can be supplied in various different ways: shapes, colours or simply text! Does the reader need to know that the needle indicates 80% on the dial or can 80% be displayed in a warning colour?

The difference in legibility between the tiny arrow in the gauge and the large number in the yellow box is marked. The text value could be reduced in size without compromising its effectiveness and would save space.

To its credit, what a gauge does provide is an upper limit. If the gauge was measuring a threat level between one and five, and it was replaced with text, then a large figure 4 isn't very informative. Four out of what? Ten? Four out of four? A gauge provides the reader with the relevant details to aid understanding.

There are two ways around this. Firstly, the scale could be so well known that there is no need to state X out of Y – movie classifications, for instance. The US system of movie ratings – G, PG, PG-13, R and NC-17 – is very well known (in the US, at least). Stating "PG-13 out of five" doesn't make sense. A similar problem plagues the star ratings we talked about in chapter 17. One way to solve this is to display empty stars so the reader knows the upper limit. So, secondly, if replacing the gauge with text, be sure to state the upper bound explicitly.

Part of the problem with using gauges and dials as alerts is that they become part of the background. If 99% of the time the needle sits in the green, the gauge isn't worth looking at; then that one per cent of the time when it is in the red, the gauge will go unnoticed. There is no need for an "everything is OK" alarm, so why have the gauge when the value is in the green? Make it appear only when there is a warning, then it's obvious when there is trouble! But now we've strayed from our subject – this is less about data and more about user interface design and human behaviour.

24 SOUND

One subject we haven't touched on is the use of senses other than sight when designing with data. None of the examples in this book make use of smell, texture, taste or sound. That's not to say you couldn't make a physical, three-dimensional version of any of these graphs for visually impaired people to understand the data.

It's pretty unlikely that we'll make a smell or taste chart any time soon. In fact, I'm not sure I'd want to smell different stocks and have their spiciness equate to upward trends and sourness equate to downward trends. Without exploring this cul-de-sac too far, there are only five basic flavours – salty, sweet, sour, bitter and umami (sometimes referred to as savoury) – which would be a problem if different flavours were assigned to different items in the chart. Like colours, variations and mixtures of the flavours would have to be used and people without sophisticated palates would get confused. Is that sour, or sweet and sour?

Sounds as data points

We can, however, experiment with sound as an medium for data. Back in chapter 3 we talked about the difference between dynamic and static charts. When dealing with sound, we are no longer in the realm of static design. Sound is dynamic information that can be played at different times with specific durations and at particular pitches.

There are several ways to encode sound. The obvious example is musical notation. The key signature, tempo, note pitches and duration are transcribed using a standardized format. This is similar to words on a page: the written music is read and understood by the musicians who then transform it into sound as they play or sing.

Methods of encoding sound can also be physical or mechanical. A vibrating needle etched sound waves on to wax cylinders to first record sound that could be played back; vinyl records work in a similar way. Now CDs, DVDs and MP3s use digital bits. There are analog equivalents to those digital ones and zeros: the old player pianos (sometimes called pianolas) whose piano rolls map the music in perforated paper; or those tiny music boxes where a toothed wheel rotates against chimes to make sounds at the correct intervals to play a tune. These are interactive but also analog.

Fractions of a Second: An Olympic Musical

At the Olympics, the blink of an eye can be all that separates the gold medalist from the 10th-place finisher. In some events, this is obvious. But in others, with athletes racing one by one, the closeness of the race is harder to perceive. Listen to the differences below.

Alpine skiing

The women's downhill course was extremely tiring, and, because it was more challenging than the men's course, it ended up separating the skiers by much larger margins. This pattern appears in the two speed events: the downhill and the super-G.

	WINNING TIME	SECONDS BEHIND GOLD MEDALIST
PLAY ▸ Women's Downhill	1:44.19	
PLAY ▸ Men's Downhill	1:54.31	
PLAY ▸ Women's Super-G	1:20.14	
PLAY ▸ Men's Super-G	1:30.34	
PLAY ▸ Women's Super Combined	2:09.14	
PLAY ▸ Men's Super Combined	2:44.92	
PLAY ▸ Women's Slalom	1:42.89	
PLAY ▸ Men's Slalom	1:39.32	
PLAY ▸ Women's Giant Slalom	2:27.11	
PLAY ▸ Men's Giant Slalom	2:37.83	

(Scale: 0, 0.25, 0.5, 0.75, 1, 1.25 seconds)

http://www.nytimes.com/interactive/2010/02/26/sports/olympics/20100226-olysymphony.html

The New York Times tried an experiment with an audio chart. It took events from the 2010 Winter Olympics and plotted the race times.

The winning athlete's time was placed at the zero point and everyone else's time was offset from this. For instance, if it took the winner 1 minute 54.31 seconds to complete the course, that becomes the zero point. If the next competitor's time was 1 minute 54.40 seconds we'd subtract the winning time from it, meaning he was 0.09 seconds behind the winner and that time would be plotted at 0.09 seconds after the zero on the timeline.

An audible beep was added for each contestant's time as a data point. Pressing play plays the series of beeps, each spaced out in time as the athletes crossed the finish line. It's an interesting way to represent the data both visually and audibly. From a graph, the reader can't feel what it's like to be 0.09 seconds behind, but from a series of notes a listener can discover how close or far apart 0.09 seconds is.

This idea could be used in many different situations. Imagine real time edits to Wikipedia as a tune. The size of the edit could adjust the pitch, so the changes in the text could be heard as a melody. If the sounds consisted of ambient noises, then you could go about your daily business until a shriek of high-pitched tones caught your ear. Those might be frequent, large edits, possibly the mark of a spammer.

I have heard of system administrators doing something similar with server activity. Instead of a dashboard of green lights and percentages of server loads (and we know how well gauges and thermometers work as charts and graphs), they switched to bird sounds. Maybe each server had a distinct bird chirp. As activity increased, the sound would go from calm to a cacophony of birdsong. At that point, the sysadmins knew something was wrong and had a look.

In certain situations, it's possible to use sound as a way to convey information behind the data and to tell a story. From Olympic medal times and wiki updates to server loads, unique uses to engage the other senses can be found.

Visualizing sound

Sound travels in waves, which can easily be visualized. We recognize a waveform shape from just about any audio app.

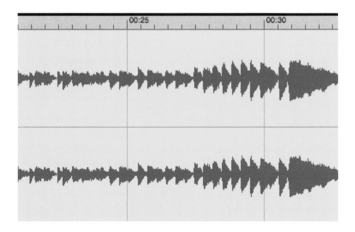

---

1   http://bza.biz/project/wavefrom-necklace/

There are peaks and valleys, dead air and noise. These waveforms are made up of hundreds of pitches and different tones. A pure tone on an oscilloscope would produce a smooth sine wave.

Some people have turned this into art and created waveform jewellery'. It is a nice way to visualize sound, but it doesn't tell us much.

Different tones have different wavelengths, each producing different vibrations in our ears and, therefore, different sounds in our brains. Waveforms are one way to visualize sound, but perhaps not the most exciting or unique. Enter Ernst Florens Friedrich Chladni.

Ernst Chladni was born in late 1756 in Germany. Like William Playfair, Chladni was a something of a polyglot. He had degrees in law and philosophy, but was more interested in physics and music. Drawing on his scientific knowledge, he researched and developed several interesting techniques in the study of sound and is sometimes referred to as the father of acoustics. He was also an early pioneer in studying meteorites and is regarded by some as the father of meteoritics, but we'll have to leave that story for another time.

In 1787 he published his *Discoveries in the Theory of Sound*, in which he describes his development of an earlier experiment by Robert Hooke (1635–1703) of Oxford University. Chladni drew a bow across a metal plate (subsequently named after him as

Chladni plates) whose surface was lightly covered with sand. The vibrations through the plate excited the sand particles and settled them into a nodal pattern caused by the sound waves. These experiments can create beautiful designs based on different pitches.

Today, these shapes are generated in much the same way except that instead of a bow a loudspeaker emitting a specific pitch is used – the effects are the same. There are plenty of videos about how these patterns are created and the mysteries surrounding them. In the Rosslyn Chapel just south of Edinburgh in Scotland, there are several designs in the stonework which look very much like these patterns. The chapel, built in the mid fifteenth century, is one of the places reputed to be the hiding place of the Holy Grail and is decorated with many cryptic symbols. A father-and-son team matched the stone Chladni patterns into their musical pitch equivalents, producing a tune they call Rosslyn Motet.

Knowledge of these patterns is used in the construction of acoustic instruments such as guitars and violins. The patterns represent complex mathematical equations and all the data points which underlie the acoustic sounds. By putting sand on the bodies and playing a particular pitch, a specific Chladni pattern should emerge. If not, then the construction and shape of the instrument are incorrect. This is an ingenious way to test the design to see if it generates the same audio data set in a consistent manner between instruments.

The study of visible sound and vibrations is referred to as cymatics. If you are interested in learning more, searching for "cymatics" or "Chladni" is an excellent starting point.

25 EVERYTHING AND THE KITCHEN SINK

Sadly, this is the last chapter and there is so much more to explore! Before we go, it's important to at least touch on a few other charts and graphs which show promise and can be adapted to uses beyond their original purpose. Once you understand what each is designed to represent and your data fits those critiera, you should feel confident in using them.

Population pyramid

The population pyramid is an uncommon type of chart that you're not likely to have come across. This isn't because it is bad, but because its use is quite specific.

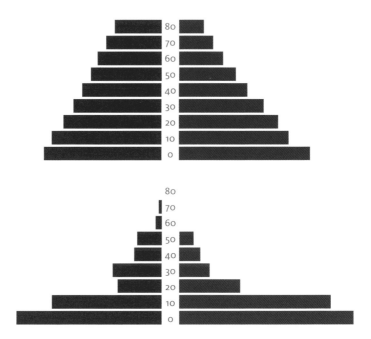

The name comes from the chart's appearance: it tends to look like a pyramid in shape. It is split vertically down the middle – in the examples, one side represents males (blue), the other females (purple). Each horizontal bar is a count of people in a particular age group. Age increases up the vertical axis with fewer and fewer people in the higher age groups.

The different shapes of the pyramid give a general overview of the population and potential troubles down the road. An aging baby boomer generation outnumbers later births. China's one child per family initiative has decimated the lower half of its pyramid. Rising child mortality rates would appear in this chart as a straighter-sided pyramid. If there was a high birth rate but few children survived past the age of five, there would be a large bulge at the bottom, with a curve upwards resembling a hockey stick.

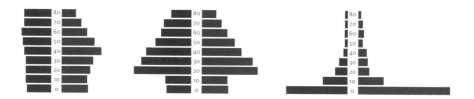

Since the pyramids are effectively two bar charts turned on their sides and placed back to back, all the benefits and weaknesses discussed in chapter 17 regarding bar charts apply. The bars are absolute values, so you can compare two different population pyramids as long as the scale is the same.

There are opportunities to replicate the framework of a population pyramid with other data types. The goal of the design is to deal with a data set over time, so this could be growth of cities each year, number of cars sold per year, and so on.

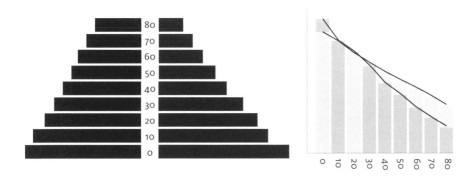

This, of course, could be designed as a line graph or regular bar chart. The pyramid aspect brings with it the opportunity to compare the two variables next to each other, just like two lines on a line graph.

Phillips curve

In 1958, the economist William Phillips wrote a paper called 'The Relationship between Unemployment and the Rate of Change of Money Wages in the United Kingdom 1861–1957'. He attempted to show an inverse relationship between unemployment and the inflation rate (when inflation is high, unemployment is low). For the article, he created a new type of chart which now bears his name: the Phillips curve.

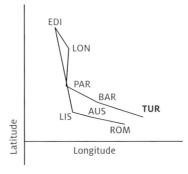

A Phillips curve is a sort of cross between a scatter plot and a line graph. The grid plots the unemployment rate on one axis and inflation or deflation on the other. This makes it similar to a scatter plot but by connecting the data points, a sort of scribbly timeline is formed.

While Phillips tried to demonstrate a specific shape in his paper, it's possible to reuse this concept in other ways. If we look back at chapter 21 about maps, we could overlay a Phillips-style curve of both time and direction to some travel plans: from London to Paris; then Paris to Madrid; Madrid to Rome, and so on. Just as the Phillips curve plots points on two axes, we can replace unemployment and inflation with latitude and longitude, then connect the points over time. This doesn't imply that latitude and longitude have a statistical relationship, but it shows that the visual characteristics of the Phillips curve can be repurposed.

One disadvantage of a Phillips curve is that it has the potential to get cluttered quickly as the line retraces itself. It is a halfway house between a scatter plot and a flow map. It isn't as heavy as a flow map with large arrows and it has an extra dimension – time – which is lacking in a scatter plot. This is another chart type to keep in your toolbox as you design with data.

Venn diagrams

It's widely believed that around 1880 John Venn – yes, he was a real person – created a way to visualize sets graphically using overlapping circles. This kicked off the field of set theory and had wider impacts in a variety of other disciplines.

Venn diagrams can be used when there are several possible relations between a finite collection of data sets. Venn diagrams quickly map out possibilities visually to help aid understanding of the logic. Let's take the statements "Humans are mammals" and "All mammals are in the animal kingdom", and ask "Is a human an animal?" Because of set theory and a string of logical statements, we can prove this true. This same chain of logic is what got Socrates killed, so I wouldn't go around at the next party spouting off. It's for your own safety, trust me.

Venn diagrams allow us to quickly identify why this is true. First, there's a box which represents everything in the universe. Inside that box is placed a circle labelled "Animal Kingdom". Within that is a smaller circle labelled "Mammals". Finally, a point labelled "Humans" is inside the mammals circle.

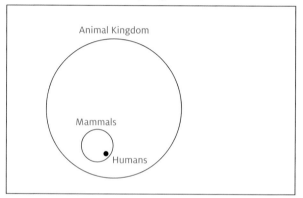

The question was, "Are humans animals?" Since the dot for humans is entirely inside the mammals circle, which is entirely inside the animal kingdom circle, then, yes, this statement is true. If the mammals circle is removed, the point for humans remains inside the animals circle.

Now let's try a slightly more complicated representation. There is a group of people who enjoy peanut butter sandwiches, a group of people who enjoy jam sandwiches and a third group of people who enjoy banana sandwiches. These are three sets of people, and there will probably be some overlap between them, since some people will eat peanut butter and jam sandwiches and others will eat banana and peanut butter sandwiches. Then there are the unfortunate people who have peanut allergies and like to eat banana and jam sandwiches.

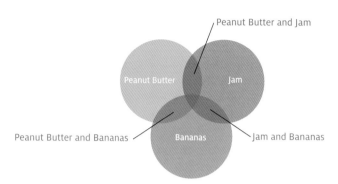

The Venn diagram allows us to more easily tell the story of who fits where and how large the overlap is between the three groups.

Creating a Venn diagram creates a visual representation of the interrelations between data. In this case, it is also a sanity check because there can't be more peanut butter and banana sandwich eaters than just plain peanut butter eaters, since every peanut butter and banana eater is also a peanut butter eater.

There are a few downsides to Venn diagrams. The overlapping shapes can become complex. Mapping out with consistency many more than three sets is difficult. Also, without labels it's difficult to judge accurately the percentage of overlap: is that a 50% or 52.45% overlap? With two arcs of two overlapping circles that may be different sizes, our mathematics might fail us.

Crop circles

I'm just sayin'! You never know! Whether hoaxes or signs of UFO invasion, crop circles registered in the world's consciousness in the 1990s. Their designs and complexity have varied over the years, probably because their creators practised more and more, or tried to out-circle the other guys. Either way, some have had incredibly mathematical and beautiful designs that it would be a shame to pass by in a book about designing with data.

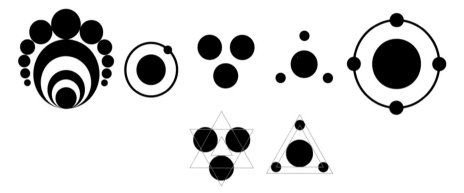

Who's to say that mathematical relationships between two ratios of objects can't be represented in other ways besides numbers? If we were trying to communicate across languages and cultures, we might need to use means other than letters and numbers. Of course, we don't need to go to another world to find someone who doesn't understand English. Is it better to label the chart Male and Female, or is it better to be language agnostic and use icons?

Some scientists have given this a lot of thought over the years. In 1977, NASA sent messages into outer space with the Voyager spacecraft with a Golden Record containing sounds and images portraying the diversity of life and culture on Earth. To explain to an extraterrestrial who has never seen a record player the actions needed to create one and at what speed to play the record required a bizarre set of instructions[1].

---

[1]   http://en.wikipedia.org/wiki/Voyager_Golden_Record

Equally as strange as the crop circles, we too have left cryptic messages to be decoded by others using the Arecibo radio telescope. In late 1974, humans beamed a message towards a star cluster some 25,000 light years away. This was the Arecibo message which was only ever sent once[1].

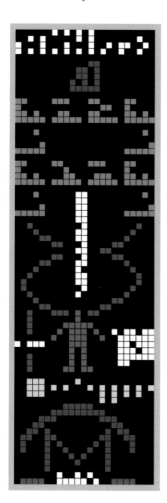

[1]   http://en.wikipedia.org/wiki/Arecibo_message

This has to qualify as one of the densest and most well thought out visualizations ever created. What was sent was a series of 1,679 ones and zeros, colour coded in this illustration to help identify the shapes. The dimensions – 23 columns by 73 rows – were chosen because they are both prime numbers. Ordering the linear stream of ones and zeros correctly makes the rectangular graphic. Each individual bit used and the total amount of bits contributes to the data of the chart itself: nothing is wasted. There is a lot to be learnt from astronomy that we can apply to our more mundane data-driven designs.

Chernoff faces

Herman Chernoff is an American mathematician born in 1923. His contribution to charts and graphs comes from the 1973 journal article, 'The Use of Faces to Represent Points in K-Dimensional Space Graphically'. Faces are interesting graphical objects. As humans, we are very good at finding tiny but distinct differences in people's faces. In those wildlife shows where naturalists know the names and faces of all the monkeys and apes they study – to me, they all look the same. Yet we don't confuse our friends or even people we've seen only once or twice – hence the phrase, "Your face looks familiar". We have an inate ability to recognize and decipher faces, and that's exactly the idea behind using Chernoff faces to describe data.

To make a Chernoff face, several pieces of data are encoded into different features. For instance, a range of zero to ten could be encoded in the width of the face: the larger the number, the wider the face. The angle of the eyebrows can be tweaked and any part of the face can be changed: nose size, hair, eyes, mouth width and how smiley it is, ears, and plenty of other characteristics. It's almost like a police identikit or Mr. Potato Head, where different parts can be swapped out depending on different values.

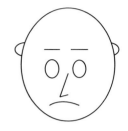

If you have a set of data with different attributes, Chernoff faces make for an excellent cross-comparison. This was done in 2008 using American baseball statistics. Each team had several attributes: wins, losses, home runs, and so on. Each of those was mapped to different parts of a face; placing them all side by side immediately revealed subtle differences.

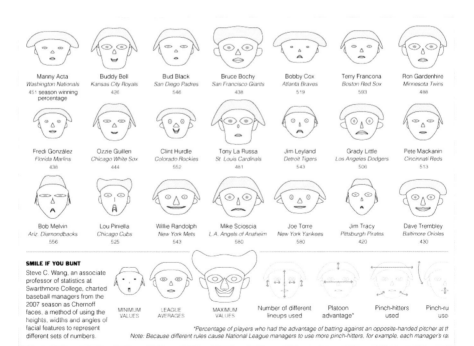

Manny Acta
Washington Nationals
451 season winning
percentage

Buddy Bell
Kansas City Royals
426

Bud Black
San Diego Padres
546

Bruce Bochy
San Francisco Giants
438

Bobby Cox
Atlanta Braves
519

Terry Francona
Boston Red Sox
593

Ron Gardenhire
Minnesota Twins
488

Fredi González
Florida Marlins
438

Ozzie Guillen
Chicago White Sox
444

Clint Hurdle
Colorado Rockies
552

Tony La Russa
St. Louis Cardinals
481

Jim Leyland
Detroit Tigers
543

Grady Little
Los Angeles Dodgers
506

Pete Mackanin
Cincinnati Reds
513

Bob Melvin
Ariz. Diamondbacks
556

Lou Piniella
Chicago Cubs
525

Willie Randolph
New York Mets
543

Mike Scioscia
L.A. Angels of Anaheim
580

Joe Torre
New York Yankees
580

Jim Tracy
Pittsburgh Pirates
420

Dave Trembley
Baltimore Orioles
430

SMILE IF YOU BUNT

Steve C. Wang, an associate professor of statistics at Swarthmore College, charted baseball managers from the 2007 season as Chernoff faces, a method of using the heights, widths and angles of facial features to represent different sets of numbers.

| MINIMUM VALUES | LEAGUE AVERAGES | MAXIMUM VALUES | Number of different lineups used | Platoon advantage* | Pinch-hitters used | Pinch-ru use |

*Percentage of players who had the advantage of batting against an opposite-handed pitcher at th
Note: Because different rules cause National League managers to use more pinch-hitters, for example, each manager's ra:

http://www.nytimes.com/2008/04/01/science/01prof.html

The face as a device to describe data works really well. It also has a fairly high data to pixel ratio because there is very little that isn't data. Edward Tufte has pointed out that a Chernoff face is symmetrical, so twice as much data is depicted than is actually required; each face could be split down the middle vertically and it would contain exactly the same information. This is true, but people respond better to a complete set of facial features.

Word clouds

If you think about it, a word cloud is similar to a pie chart: all the words in the cloud are displayed at relative sizes to each other. This means that word clouds suffer from many of the same problems as pie charts. It's difficult to compare two word clouds. The largest word in one cloud could be the same size as the largest word in another, but their respective absolute values could be levels of magnitude apart. The sizes of words are relative only within a single cloud, just as a 50% wedge in a pie chart can't yield an absolute count when comparing it to a second pie chart.

That said, word clouds do have advantages over pie charts in that it is clear when one section stops and another starts. A word cloud can contain many more words than a pie chart can have wedges; a pie chart that has 360 wedges would be ridiculous, but a word cloud of 360 words has the potential to be very information dense.

The same colour can be reused without the concern that two items would get confused. This allows the addition of a second variable into the mix, making the design of a tag cloud similar to that of a tree map. It can show both relative size and a second variable by adjusting the colour. For instance, green words might be trending up whereas red words might be trending down. A large red word could indicate that in the last time period it would have appeared even larger; a large green word could indicate that it is on the rise.

When dealing with relative values, the shapes also need to be relative. As we saw in chapter 11, when an item's height and width are doubled in two dimensions its area is squared; in three dimensions the volume is cubed. If one word cloud's largest word set in a 72 point font is the word 'boy' and a second word clould's largest 72 point word is 'onomatopoeia', there is a mismatch in the relative lengths. The height may be the same, but the area each word covers is vastly different. This makes longer words appear to have a greater weight in the given context.

If we look at the data to pixel ratio for a word cloud, it has to be one of the highest possible. There are no additional pixels that describe the chart. Each one is used in conveying information. Every drop is used in conveying information. This is both a word cloud's great advantage and its downfall. Without any sort of scale, it is nearly impossible to cross-reference and extract the numeric values that are hidden in the design.

Word clouds are relatively new, as the software needed to dynamically generate the sizes and prevent overlapping has only recently become mainstream. Time will tell if word clouds can find a seat at the adult charts and graphs table, or if they will be relegated to the children's table, forever used as a filler and friend only to the doughnut chart.

Summary

This is the end of our journey through the world of common and not so common charts and graphs. In the first three parts of this book, we laid the foundations for designing with the data. In the final two parts, we talked about the specifics.

We've come a long way since discussing the first pie chart ever created to knowing the ins and outs of some of the craziest and least useful graphs you've probably ever seen. But that's all been part of the plan. You need to know what works and, more importantly, what doesn't.

These designs are always evolving. There was a time before population pyramids and word clouds, even before bar charts and pie charts. As the landscape shifts with time and fashion, you need to recognize what works and what doesn't, as well as which tools are best for telling a particular kind of story based on the data. This is why it is important to understand both the common and uncommon graphs and charts. Any new chart development will most likely be an offshoot of an existing design, all of which have their good and bad points.

Conclusion

This book is about how to design the data so that it tells a story, enlightens your readers and helps to them to make informed decisions.

At this point, you should be not only capable of spotting bad chart design, but have the tools and knowledge to correct it. We've taken quite a journey since the first page. You now have the ability to go out and create extraordinary designs using data.

As you sit down to illustrate that next chart, ask yourself a few simple questions:

- What am I trying to convey? Will my design achieve that?
- Is this the right chart? Is the data time-sensitive? Are we looking at only a part or the whole picture?
- Is there anything that I can remove and have the graph still tell the same story?
- Are the colours usable? Will this be printed in black and white? What if the audience has problems with colour?
- Did I label the chart data and provide a title for it?

As homework, you should continue to practise creating better charts and graphs using the tips you have learnt in this book. Take an everyday item like your phone bill and try to make a better visualization from the table of data: who you called, how often and for how long are all possible variables to graph. What is the story behind those boring numbers? Once you start creating graphs, you'll come to understand your mistakes and gradually improve your skills. Don't be afraid to try different approaches.

You might not realize it, but one of the greatest charts we've all seen is under constant scrutiny. In 1869, a Russian chemist named Dmitri Mendeleev sat down with an ordered list of data. Each item in this list had a numeric value that was sequential, but at the same time there were clusters of attributes that could also be grouped. Mendeleev struggled for a long time to find the best order for the items in this list until he noticed a number of interesting patterns in the data. These patterns led him to believe that there might be some pieces missing from his list, a controversial notion in its own right. He also realized that by reconfiguring the list as a table, some of the patterns would be resolved. In laying out the list in this new way, he created the periodic table of elements that we're all familiar with. One hundred and fifty years have passed since the original seeds were sown and the periodic table's format remains the same. Every once in a while people try to improve on the design, some more successfully than others.

If you consider that people are still trying to improve a chart 150 years after its invention, you should appreciate that your design isn't really finished either. It just goes to show that there is always room for improvement.

You need to remember that visualizations and infographics aren't just buzzwords. At one point in time they were just attempts to create denser and more information-rich illustrations. Many of them fail, annoy and just plain confuse. You are now knowledgeable in the foundations of designing with data. From here, you can extend your abilities into more complex and richer visualizations. I deliberately did not cover them in this book; you need to learn how to walk before you can run and with only twenty-five chapters, we're just skimming the surface of the basics. With practice, hard work and a lot of pondering, you can become an expert. By all means, try to create some infographics; just remember everything you've read here. It all still applies, and if I find out that you are using doughnut charts, I'll hunt you down.

Remember, the goal of any chart is to tell a certain story. If a picture is worth a thousand words, then a properly designed chart is worth a thousand words multiplied by the data to pixel ratio, plus some constant, plus a really large number to sound important, and why not square that in the process? Just like any good book has a beginning, middle and end, a chart needs an introduction through its title, axes, and labels, a middle which is the data, and an end which helps the reader towards a logical conclusion. Maybe the chart makes a statement, demonstrating an imbalance or a worrying prediction; no matter what it is, you are putting yourself into the design. You have chosen the story, the data, what to show and what not to. It's your duty to eliminate confusion and to be as open and honest as possible with the results.

As a memento, I've created a special PDF file which outlines the pros and cons of each of the major chart types. You can print this out and keep it as a handy reference. It will help you decide which charts and graphs to select in which situations. It is something only for the people who have purchased this book as a cheatsheet to remind you of everything you've read.

http://designingwithdata.com/select.pdf

I'm looking forward to seeing your creations and improving, in my own small way, the thousands of charts and graphs printed every day.